THE "GILLS"
by TONY CONWAY

NEW BROMPTON FOOTBALL CLUB.
SEASON — 1905-6.

- F. GRIFFITHS, GOAL.
- J. WALTON, BACK.
- W. B. FLOYD, BACK.
- E. H. LLOYD, HALF BACK RIGHT.
- A. WEBB, BACK.
- J. MARTIN, HALF BACK.
- A. CROMBIE, DIRECTOR.
- F. GODDEN, DIRECTOR.
- F. PEARCE, DIRECTOR.
- A. W. PARKER, DIRECTOR.
- J. ELLIOTT, HALF BACK LEFT.
- F. MAVIN, HALF BACK.
- ALDERMAN J. BARNES, CHAIRMAN.
- HIS WORSHIP THE MAYOR OF GILLINGHAM, Lt. Col. J. B. RIDOUT, PRESIDENT.
- COUNCILLOR G. C. SWAIN, HON. TREASURER.
- A. BULL, HALF BACK.
- J. SHERIDAN, INSIDE RIGHT.
- W. J. GROOMBRIDGE, GENL. SECRETARY.
- W. F. PATON, HON. DOCTOR.
- A. BEADSWORTH, INSIDE LEFT.
- A. J. BURNS, OUTSIDE RIGHT.
- T. HILL, JUNR., DIRECTOR.
- W. H. CHECKFIELD, DIRECTOR.
- F. EVANS, DIRECTOR.
- W. MARRIOTT, OUTSIDE LEFT.
- E. W. SNELLGROVE, CENTRE.
- P. BARNFATHER, FORWARD.
- P. TRAVERS, FORWARD.
- J. McKEE, C. FORWARD.
- F. CRADDOCK, TRAINER.
- C. EVANS, C. FORWARD.
- H. PHILLIPS, C. FORWARD.

THE "GILLS"
by TONY CONWAY

Photographs by Roger Hills with Alan Cuff and Tess May.
Statistics provided by Roger Triggs.

Meresborough Books

7 STATION ROAD, RAINHAM, GILLINGHAM, KENT. ME8 7RS

1980

The Author, envious of his neighbour's tea.

Roger in action.

© Copyright 1980 Tony Conway

ISBN 0905270 26 6

Printed and bound by Tonbridge Printers Ltd., Tonbridge, Kent.

Introduction

I was in the Sudan some years ago. Taking a wrong road in the outskirts of Khartoum, I arrived at a picturesque bungalow and upon asking directions was presented to an Englishman who had lived in Africa for ten years or more. Over tea, our conversation naturally strayed to football and I was informed in no uncertain terms that "There's only one team for me. Gillingham. I've never seen them play mind you, but I was born in Chatham and the family, especially my Father, lived and died for the 'Gills'. During the season I really look forward to the Sunday Papers to see how we got on".

About five years later on moving to the Medway area I met many Gillingham supporters, all of whom had the same attitude as the ex-patriot Englishman. It was always 'We' when the team was referred to; they were part of the team. When the team lost, they lost; when being drawn in the F.A. Cup it was they who were apprehensive, elated, nervous and so on just as much as the players.

I decided to watch the Gills (just once or twice mind you), but like the others became 'hooked' very quickly and my relationship with the Club was cemented with a positively heroic performance on their part in the game against Swindon in 1979, when with ten men they fought superbly, draining me of adrenaline and crystalising my football loyalties. After that game I felt that 'something' should be written about a club which, after 87 years, is still the only real team in Kent.

Initially the idea was to write a simple technical text book, but as my research got under way and more and more help came from supporters I felt that I would attempt to use the book as a vehicle in creating a bridge between supporters and clubs. In addition I ascertained that a book about any football club, is, in effect, a chapter of English Social History but sadly I was not able to devote as much time to this aspect as I would have liked.

Many thanks of course to the Club and Officials for their assistance and who suffered my presence and interruptions whilst trying to get on with their jobs. To Roger Triggs with his immense knowledge of the Club's history and who as a school boy fanatic prepared the first written work on the Club back in 1972. His extremely hard work both then and now have saved me hours of toil. To The Chatham News, The Royal Navy, The Royal Engineers Librarian, plus the numerous supporters who assisted with information, old programmes and ideas. To Jan who typed. To John and Sean who constructively mocked, and to Charlotte and Magda for reasons which have to remain a secret.

Lastly to Annette, for months of understanding, gallons of coffee and constant friendship. . . her only complaint "that chain smoking is not tax deductible!"

Excelsior Football Club 1892-3
Winners of the Kent County Junior Cup, Luton Senior Cup, and Chatham District League
W.J. Murray (Secretary), A. Champness, B. Ashdown, T. Steel, J. Pearson, W. Checksfield (President)
A. Jenner, F. Manning, D. Hutcheson (Sub Captain), A. Beard (Captain), H. Buckland, W. Day.
G. Wimble, H. Tyler.

The team 1979-80
John Sharpe, Mark Weatherley, John Shaw, John Overton, Andy Ford
Alan Hodgekinson, Micky Barker, Dean White, Gary Sutton, Colin Duncan, Charlie Young, Ron Hillyard,
Steve Bruce, Nigel Donn, Bill Collins
Danny Westwood, Damien Richardson, Ken Price, Gerry Summers, Peter Henderson, Kevin Lloyd, John Crabbe
Terry Jolly, Pat Walker, Micky Adams, Tony Bottiglieri

Chapter 1

The origins of football are murky. Sustained research shows that around 200 B.C. a game with a spherical object was played in China, emphasis being placed on the art of dribbling, and records exist indicating ball games (which at a stretch of the imagination could be called the precursors of the modern game) were played by Ancient Greeks and Roman Legionaries. To look at the history of the game, some say however, is not terribly rewarding; place a ball or round object of any sort at the feet of a child (of either sex) and they will kick it.

In Britain as early as 1314 Edward II issued a proclaimation banning the game and for the next three hundred and fifty years Royal and Parliamentary efforts were made to curtail the ever popular "foolish game". Edward III in 1363 wrote to the Lord Lieutenant of Kent; "... we ordain that you prohibit under penalty of imprisonment all and sundry from such stone, wood and iron throwing; hand ball, football or hockey; courting and cockfighting; or other idle games". Again in 1583 an Elizabethan writer castigated the sport stating (I am using modern English) 'I protest now to you. It may be called rather a friendly fight than play or recreation. A bloody practice not a friendly sport or pastime for is it not true to say that one lies in wait for one's adversary seeking him and punch him on the nose and many have their necks, backs, legs and arms broken. Nobody goes scot free but they are either wounded, grazed, bruised, gashed against the ground, hit with elbows, punched with gripped fist, kneed, all of which leads to envy, malice, rancour, hatred, displeasure, enmity, fighting, brawling, contention, quarrel picking, murder, homicide and a great effusion of blood. Is this a Christian dealing for one brother to maim and hurt another?'

The game, if it can be called a game, really served as an outlet for the rivalries of adjoining villages where the abled bodied males would turn out in an effort to kick or carry a ball from one village to the other. In reality the sport was an amalgum of our present day rugby and football; a dash of all-in-wrestling, a modicum of boxing, some karate, plus a few hundred yard sprints.

For reasons unknown (perhaps the Draconian penalties imposed upon players?) the labouring classes 'grew tired' of the sport and gave it up. Ironically, at the same time it became of interest to the then Upper Class who took the historical relay baton, and in the change over transformed it from wood to bronze. Later individuals would transform it to gold.

The starting point for soccer 'proper' is generally agreed upon as being about the middle of the nineteenth century when rules of sorts came to be accepted and players formed themselves into the recognised club system. The first football club in Britain (and most probably the world) was inaugurated in Sheffield during 1856 when 'Old Boys' of the Universities got together to try and standardise the sport, their efforts finally leading to the formation of the Football Association in 1863 under what was known as the Cambridge University Rules. Initiated, if that is the correct word, by the Public Schools, the 'agreed' game was a mixture of our present day rugby and soccer. Slowly the sport 'filtered downwards' and small local clubs sprang up, playing wherever they could find a ground of adequate size.

But when we talk about the early years it must be borne in mind that the rules of the game prior to the 1870's would be unrecognisable to us today. For example the goalkeeper, as we know him, came into being around 1870 and was '... the player, who for the time being is nearest to his own goal' (a sort of rush goalie!) Again that friend of all fans the referee did not appear officially until 1871 for it was an accepted tradition of those times that when Gentlemen from Public Schools and Universities played soccer unfair advantage would not be taken and thus an umpire was superfluous. Even when a referee did come into being he did not have a whistle until 1878 and one tries to imagine such a person shouting his instructions to players. "I say... I say... excuse me, yes you with the handlebar moustache... Johnson isn't it?... it seemed to me as if the ball went out of play off your knee. . . I say old chaps would you lot stop kicking the ball over there whilst I'm talking to Mr Johnson here about a throw in. . ."

As with most things, historians disagree on how the name Gillingham came about. I am prepared to accept, on balance, that the best suggestion is from the Saxon words Gylla (pond) Ham (village). What is in a name however? To most people throughout the British Isles the town of Gillingham is almost unknown. Perhaps it is even fairer to state that it is totally unknown save for the fact that some twenty million or so football supporters regularly see it when they read the results on a Saturday. The point to be made is the affect which a football club has upon a town. Throughout the Country clubs such as Gillingham exist, not as independent units but as part of the town, its people and culture.

The embryo of the present establishment in Priestfield Road was a very successful local club known as Excelsior. Sadly, due to the hazy references made to it in the Press and the lack of adquate records, little is known of its background. In 1910 a Football League Book suggests, in a chapter written by William Ironside Groombridge (at that time the Secretary of New Bromptom), "there can be no doubt that the military element have by example and precept taught the youth of New Bromptom how to appreciate field sports, manly pastimes and athletic exercises generally". The Royal Engineers stationed in the area since the Napoleonic War obviously had an affect on soccer in the Gillingham area although not too much emphasis should be placed on this. In 1893 a motion was put forward by the Royal Engineers Football Club that the name of the club be changed from Royal Engineers Football Club to Royal Engineers Officers Football Club. Captain Thackwell said "outsiders naturally inferred that the club was made up of the Royal Engineers at large. The club was started for Officers and therefore only Officers should play". Some corporal or private of outstanding ability had been sneaked into the team and the general feeling of the meeting was that this should be stopped. The name of the club was not changed, but the Captain of the team was given a slight rap on the knuckles. At that time still there was a deep division between what could be termed the 'official' footballers (Public Schools/Universities/Officer Corps) and local teams.

However one cannot but accept Groombridge's view that the Engineers, with their team made up of men from all over the British Isles, was outstanding during the latter part of the 19th century, and by its mere existence encouraged the locals to partipate in the game. It is worth looking at that team which lost only three games over four years! The record is as follows:— played 86, won 74, lost 3 (two of them cup finals in 1872 and 1874) drew 9. Goals for: 244 — against 21. Organised by Sir Francis Marindin, perhaps one of the greatest technicians of the game and the first to appreciate it as a team game, he twice led his team to the F.A. Cup Final but was sadly absent from the winning side in 1875. But not only did he create a 'Superteam of the Seventies', he also loved the game and its lore; he wanted more than just to play and enjoy the physical aspects of the game. Taking part in all facets of the sport he acted as referee in eight Cup Finals and in 1871 was part of the committee which inaugurated the F.A. Cup, in which he was to play such a great part. Eventually, as a result of his skill and enthusiasm he became President of the Football Association (1874-1890).

So in the Medway Towns there existed between 1872 and 1878 a team which was unbeatable, but, as Groombridge says ". . . while the R.E.'s and their Star Visitors had their followers, the local clubs were not wanting for their supporters. . . the small local clubs of those days, who also played on the Great Lines were to be found trying pluckily to adopt the tactics of the famous. . . such clubs as Victoria, St. Marks and Excelsior were in the front of local football".

An unknown reporter of the time records one of the many games played on the Great Lines during the Excelsior period. "There is a downward slope towards the picturesque and well known River Medway which is apt to cause the game to be somewhat one sided at any rate in one sense of the word; also the goal posts at one end of the ground are in close proximity to a manure heap. . . so that unless the goalkeeper wears some sort of respirator over his nose and mouth it is a dead certainty he will be sick."

Manure heaps and slanted pitches notwithstanding, the national upsurge in the game continued amongst all classes of the population which in due course led to a meeting of Excelsior supporters and backers taking place at the 'Napier Arms', Brompton in 1893.

Chapter 2

1893 was the year when Mao-Tse-Tung, Herman Goring and the New Brompton Football Club were born.

By then a distinct change had taken place in the game. In the Cup Final of 1891/2, West Bromwich Albion had beaten Aston Villa in front of 32,000 people who had paid £1,757 to see the game. Not professional in the true sense of the word football was becoming a sport which could prove profitable, although this is not to decry the philanthropic approach of local businessmen who became involved in those days.

Regular discussions of football committees had occurred in the 'Napier Arms', for some time (possibly since 1865) and there, in the comfort of the 'Snug' (and no doubt lubricated against the cold and pessimistic thoughts) local businessmen considered the idea of putting a football team on a more formalised basis. As supporters and enthusiasts for Excelsior, they would have been on the crest of a wave, as their team had just won the Kent Junior Cup and the Chatham District League without losing a single match.

Accordingly a meeting was arranged for the 18th May 1893 when the following gentlemen were elected to promote a football company. James Barnes (Licensed Victualler), Frederick Bloor (Wardrobe Dealer), William Checksfield (Licensed Victualler), Horace Croneen (Jeweller), Walter Croneen (Licensed Victualler), Henry Elliott (Builder), Albert Partridge (Station Master), Richard Passby (Wine Merchant), George Randall (Pawnbroker), Alfred Richardson (Sergeant: Royal Engineers), William Snow (Builder) and Edwin Warren (Medical Practitioner).

A few days later the parties made efforts to decide on the name of their new club, which in effect was an extension of Excelsior. Bloor and Barnes suggested 'The New Brompton Athletic Ground Company Ltd'. Elliott and Partridge in turn thought 'New Brompton Football and Athletic Ground Company Ltd' was a better suggestion. Richardson and Checksfield came in with 'New Brompton Football Club Co. Ltd'. Debate ensued and Richardson and Checksfield were successful. The next step was to find a place to play and investigations were put under way culminating in three distinct choices on which the final 'a section of land in Gillingham Road close to the level crossing' at a cost of £600.00 was accepted. Arrangements then had to be made to purchase clothing, select players, print tickets and so on. £10 was paid for a turnstile and it was agreed to buy Brodies Patented Goal Nets. An argument ensued on the 4th August, 1893 as to what type of goal posts were to be purchased. Elliott and Checksfield stated that "three inches by three inches was sufficient". However Croneen and Partridge disagreed and thought "four and a half inches by three inches would be better" and their view prevailed. Then came intense discussions on the type of lawnmower to be used, was it to be sixteen inches or twenty four inches? The votes were even in this crucial debate, the Chairman giving his casting vote in favour of a sixteen inch lawnmower. Next on the Agenda to occupy the Directors' minds was the question of 'flannel shirts, stockings and knickers'! Sadly no tape recordings are available of the depth of feeling on these subjects.

Mr Walter Hurst had presented a flagstaff to the Company in early September ready for the first game on the 9th which no doubt gave the ground some dignity and I can do no better than quote a report in the Chatham and Rochester News of the first match day. "The 'Colony' of New Brompton is laudably ambitious and kingly desirous to at least keep abreast of its neighbours . . . It possesses a Technical Institute which ere long will be open to Students; it has a safe dock. . . the foundation work for a new pier goes on slowly but surely, to crown it all, a football ground has actually been purchased and laid out, the first matches on which were played on Saturday. At present the ground is well away from dwelling houses, but the 'brick and mortar mania' is highly

CHATHAM AND ROCHESTER NEWS, SATURDAY, MAY 13, 1893

NEW BROMPTON FOOTBALL CLUB.

IMPORTANT MEETING AT THE NAPIER ARMS.

Is it possible and practicable that the New Brompton football enthusiasts shall have a ground of their own, to centralise and encourage local players, and to run the club on democratic lines as well as make it pay? That question—not a slight one by the way—is at present occupying intense attention at New Brompton, and has been the object of many meetings. Time will show anyway, judging from the size of the meeting held at the Napier Arms on Wednesday evening last, the multiplicity of ideas, and yet withal the unanimity that prevailed, if the scheme is not successful it certainly deserves success. By the unanimous wish of the meeting, Dr. E. C. Warren, C.C., was called upon to preside, and his supporters included Messrs. H. G. Croneen, W. Murray (sec.), J. Barnes, A. Stride, H. Nye, R. Thompson, W. C. Snow, W. H. Checksfield, A. W. Partridge, G. B. Winch, W. Croneen, H. W. Elliot, T. Hibbard, C. Fynn, jun., F. Bonny, P. Luff, E. J. Goodwin, J. Pierson, A. Beard, F. Lipop, Davis, P. Little, W. Packer, F. Bloor, Jenner, C. Wellard, A. Borer, B. F. Corbett, W. Vincent, W. Manning, &c.

As one of the committee appointed at the last meeting, Mr. R. Thompson reported having waited on Mr. Webb, but as a price was not definitely proposed by that gentleman, and neither could terms for leasing his land be arranged, the matter was so far in abeyance. Mr. Elliott submitted to the meeting a plan of a piece of ground situated on the Beacon Court estate, with a frontage to Byron-road and Rock-avenue. He entered into the details of the probable cost, and the terms on which the ground—about 6½ acres—could be acquired, and how it might be advantageously secured for the club.

The meeting, later on, resolved that for the immediate present, prices should not be publicly discussed, so these figures with others were allowed to stand over for future consideration.

Several gentlemen remarked on the advantages of the central situation of the Beacon Court site.

Mr. Hammond also came armed with a plan of a site which he submitted to the meeting, in Barnsole-lane, just above Mr. Green's house. This piece of ground has the advantage of being nearly level, the fall being only one foot in 190. If the club wished to purchase a plot and this as regards size was ample for their purpose—no doubt at a reasonable price it could be obtained. He thought that in the long run they would find it more profitable to go in for direct purchase than to take ground on a lease, for by that means they avoided the risk of being thrown out when the lease expired. They would also not be exactly restricted to the amount shown on the plan, for if they secured this plot and at a future date required to enlarge it, the adjoining land, he might say, could be secured. Mr. Hammond entered into various details as to cost, but Mr. Croneen, in the interests of the club, proposed that they be not now gone into, for if it was made public that they really wanted a certain piece, they would have "to pay through the nose for it."

Mr. Partridge seconded this, and the meeting acquiesced.

From the various amounts that accidentally did slip out in the observations made by various speakers (which sums varied from £600 to £1,200), showing that specific ideas were not quite unanimous, there was no doubt a wise resolution.

Mr. Croneen then laid on the table a plan of piece of ground in Gillingham-road, near the level crossing and opposite to Mrs. Steel's residence. He pointed out that for shape and size this piece would suit admirably. It was more than sufficient for a regulation plot for football and would allow of a cycle track round it. I was hedged on two sides, so that less boarding would be required. Of course they must be guided by circumstances, and select what they considered would be the best site.

With Messrs. Webb and Bryant's piece, which many of the younger members at the meeting seemed most sweet on, there were thus four plans before the meeting.

Dr. Warren asked if they intended to enter for the All England Cup? This drew forth a unanimous "yes"; then, said the Doctor, the point of depending on hedges must be dropped, as the Association would insist on having the ground properly enclosed.

Here the discussion drifted into the question as to whether a football ground could be utilized for cricket. Without entering into the pros and cons of this point it was left with the statement that it would, after the rough wear of the winter be totally unfit for cricket, but would make a splendid tennis ground, and that a spirited competition might be expected amongst local tennis players to secure some part of it.

Mr. Hammond and Mr. Winch also addressed the meeting on the point of the estimated time it would take to prepare a ground. The properties of lucerne, grass seed, &c., came prominently to the fore, but as the majority were not well coached up in the subject, that too was left for future settlement.

Mr. Winch, in a clear and practical speech, pointed out the two courses they might adopt, of either securing a site on a lease and getting a number of gentlemen to guarantee a sum of money to defray the initial expenses, or to float a company to secure the ground and then let it to the Football Club. In either case they would have to study the financial side of the question. Putting the population of Gillingham at 30,000, and say one-fifth of them were men, only about a half of whom they could expect to regularly attend their matches, this gave them a 3,000 gate, and could they afford to bring important clubs to New Brompton when they could only anticipate such support as this. He did not wish to throw cold water on the idea, but the question of preliminary costs, future expenses, and probable returns must be considered (cheers).

Mr. A. Beard thought that Mr. Webb's plan had not been thoroughly explained. Personally, he should advocate getting if possible the plot above the tunnel.

Mr. E. J. Goodwin also advocated this site, because of its central position to New Brompton, Luton, and Chatham.

Dr. Warren remarked that they must get a ground, or where could they take these good clubs they were anxious to see, when they did come.

Mr. T. Hibberd hoped they would be able to form a company; the idea of asking for guarantors was not a very popular one; he also hoped that a large number of gentlemen interested in the game would be induced to take up shares.

Mr. Checksfield wanted to see some of the "bunce" go to the players.

Mr. R. T. Thompson proposed that a limited liability company be formed with £1 shares.

Mr. H. G. Croneen seconded this, and, after a lengthy discussion, in which Mr. B. F. Corbett and Mr. Lipop took part, it was carried.

Mr. Lipop pointed out that they must appoint a governing body to carry out the initial workings. He thought that they had proceeded in the right direction, for when it went forth that a company was formed it would carry greater weight and be the more likely to secure success.

A provisional committee and officers were then appointed as follows:—Chairman, Mr. H. G. Croneen; Secretary, Mr. W. Murray; committee, Messrs. W. C. Snow, R. Thompson, A. W. Partridge, H. W. Elliott, W. Croneen, A. Parker, A. Beard, J. Barnes, P. Little, W. H. Checksfield, Steel, A. Buckland, W. Manning, W. Crump, and E. J. Goodwin.

It was decided to call the next meeting on Thursday week, at the Napier Arms.

A vote of thanks to the Chairman closed the meeting.

At a public meeting held at the Napier Arms Inn New Brompton, this day, to consider the question of the formation of a Company to be called the New Brompton Football Club Ground Comp'y Limited

It was proposed by Mr. H. G. Croneen, seconded by Mr. Crump that the High Constable of Gillingham (W. R. Featherby Esq.) take the Chair

The Minutes of the last meeting were passed as read.

Mr. H. G. Croneen as Chairman of a Committee nominated to view and report upon various sites offered to the Company having read his report It was proposed by Mr. Partridge and seconded by Mr. Reed that Mr. Lipop's tender be read with the others

Proposed as an Amendment by Mr. Parker and seconded by Mr. W. Croneen that it be not entertained
 There voted for the amendment 22
 For the original proposition — 30

Tenders having been read by Mr. H. G. Croneen It was proposed by Mr. Passby seconded by Mr. Richardson that the tender of Mess'r Tilley & Randall be accepted. Carried.

Proposed by Mr. Thompson seconded by Mr. P. Little that the following Gentlemen be elected a Committee to promote the Company

Mr. James Barnes of The Railway Hotel New Brompton Licensed Victualler

Mr. Frederick Bloor of High Street New Brompton Wardrobe dealer

Mr. William Herbert Checksfield of The Napier Arms Inn New Brompton Licensed Victualler

Mr. Horace George Croneen of High Street New Brompton Jeweller

Mr. Walter Croneen of The Viscount Hardinge Inn New Brompton

Mr. Henry William Elliot of Napier Road New Brompton Builder

Mr. Albert William Partridge of New Brompton Station Master

Mr. Richard James Passby of Beacon Court Canterbury Road New Brompton Wine Merchant

Mr. George Randall of High Street New Brompton Pawnbroker

Mr. Alfred Concannon Richardson of Windmill Road New Brompton Quarter Master Sergeant R.E.

Mr. William Cornish Snow of Canterbury Street New Brompton Builder

Edwin Charles Warren Esq High Street New Brompton Medical Practitioner

Proposed by Mr. H. G. Croneen Seconded by Mr. Evans that the High Constable of Gillingham for the time being be President of the New Brompton Football Club.

      Chairman

The first two pages in the minute books, dated 18th May 1893.

The New Brompton Football Club
Winners of the Charity Cup 1893-4
W. Murray, A. Jenner, J. Taylor, H. Auld, G. Liddle
C. Hibbard, A. Ashdown, D. Hutcheson (Captain), H. Buckland, A. James.
H. Tyler, M. Rowlands.

contagious and no doubt ere long houses will crop up all around the enclosure. Even on Saturday one individual saved threepence by viewing the matches from a roof at least three hundred yards away.

"Our representative was directed to make for the New Brompton Railway Station, across the bridge, walk down Franklin Road, turn to the right, then to the left, go up a road, cross a meadow and then he would arrive at his destination. Happily he met with Mr. Director, J. Randall, a gentleman who had so devoted himself to the task of getting the ground ready for the fray that on Friday his better half despatched his dinner and tea to the football ground, whether hammock also found its way thither report sayeth not. Under the guidance of the 'bread man' the route was easy, and on their way Mr. Referee, W. Roberts, was overtaken; others joined them . . . and arrived at the turnstiles. How many of the group had paid for admission doesn't concern anybody — the magic word 'Season' was apparently the password and the ground was entered. Here everything was of the newest, even the grass, in fact there had not been time to indulge in the luxury of paint; but a little powder there may have been, as ladies mustered a strong force, and they do sometimes use 'just a little' you know. Finishing touches were being put here and there and 'Mein Host' of the 'Napier Arms' was making ready for his share in the day's proceedings —

not inconsiderably as events turned out, and Mr. Chairman, H. G. Croneen, at last triumphantly exclaimed "Now we are ready for them." Spectators dropped in by twos and threes until some 500 were present to witness the first match."

By November potential employees were being interviewed and at the same time two tons of coconut fibre was purchased. Initially I could not conceive why this had occurred until it was pointed out to me by an erudite friend that pitches also got waterlogged in 1893! Efforts were at that time being made to arrange games with other small teams such as Tottenham Hotspur, Woolwich Arsenal and Millwall. Correspondence ensued between the new club and these other clubs suggesting guarantee fees which in the case of a senior team like Millwall could be as high as £20 although in the case of the lesser clubs such as Tottenham Hotspur only £7.10s. was suggested.

By 1894 the Directors had got into the swing of running a football club, making protests, receiving deputations, interviewing propective players and naturally enough dealing with the problem of hooliganism. In particular the Police were instructed to stop horn blowing on the ground.

CHATHAM AND ROCHESTER NEWS, SATURDAY, FEBRUARY 17, 1894.

NEW BROMPTON v. SWINDON TOWN

NEW BROMPTON VICTORIOUS BY TWO GOALS TO ONE.

Owing to the executive of the New Brompton Club sending their "A" team to Rochester to represent them against the City team, it left the first "string" without a fixture, but fortunately at the eleventh hour, or nearly so, Swindon Town were induced to fill the breach. The afternoon was fine, but for the third Saturday in succession a high westerly wind prevailed, and rendered good and accurate football at a discount, and also had a telling effect on the "gate," only about fifteen hundred spectators having the courage to face the elements. The Railway town contingent were not at full strength, being minus four of their cup team. The "Colonials" were thoroughly represented. Ashdown (having recovered from an attack of influenza, which kept him out of the team against Burton Swifts) again partnering Auld at back, whilst Rowlands was included in the front rank, vice McIntosh. A start was effected soon after the advertised time, the teams being in the following order:—

Swindon Town—C. Williams (goal), H. Vowles and W. Richardson (backs), J. M. Parker, W. Mantell, and H. Spackman (half-backs), R. Reynolds and R. H. Davies (captain) (right wing), A. Andrews (centre), D. Mahoney and J. Hayward (left wing).

New Brompton—J. Taylor (goal), M. Auld and A. Ashdown (backs), G. Liddle, A. James, and H. Tyler (half-backs), M. Rowlands and H. Buckland (left wing), D. Hutcheson (captain) (centre), C. Hibbard and A. Jenner (right wing).

Referee.—Mr. W. Roberts (New Brompton). Linesmen.—Messrs. J. Williams (Swindon Town), and W. J. Murray (New Brompton).

SWINDON HAVE THE BETTER OF THE ARGUMENT IN THE FIRST HALF.

It fell to the lot of the visiting captain (Davies) to win the toss, and he gave his team the benefit of playing with the wind and sun behind them for the first forty-five minutes. Swindon were not long before they became dangerous, Andrews being dispossessed by Ashdown in front of goal, and a fine long shot from Spackman was also attended to by "Buck." Buckland got possession and made tracks for the other end, but an attempted pass to Rowlands was intercepted by Vowles, who cleared with a huge kick. Hayward was the next to become dangerous, and eluded Tyler, but failed to trick Ashdown, who kept him off the ball, whilst Auld cleared. An abortive corner fell to the visitors, and then Brompton attacked all along the line, but again Vowles was in evidence, and stopped the incursion. After the Swindon men had taken a couple of unproductive corners, they scored in a most unexpected and easy manner. Hayward, the outside left, essayed a shot, and Auld tried to keep Spackman off the sphere and allow it to roll into touch. In this he failed, and Taylor, seeing danger, rushed out and kicked the ball unluckily against Auld, with the result that it rebounded off the back and into the goal, this occurring after a quarter of an hour's play. On the resumption, Mahoney had a capital chance, but was hampered, and was obliged to kick the ball wide. The Swindonians, aided by the wind, had the best of the play, but the Brompton halves and backs were in fine fettle, and frustrated all their efforts. By the exertions of Hibbard, Jenner, and Hutcheson, the siege was transferred to the other end, and Rowlands was given an opportunity, but his shot sailed over the bar. A free kick for hands against Mantell was of little use to the Brompton lads, and Swindon securing, were soon troubling the home defence. James proved their stumbling block, and placed nicely to Buckland, who in turn transferred to Hutcheson, but the home captain held the ball too long, and Vowles cleared. Buckland and Hutcheson were next conspicuous for some pretty passing, and on nearing the uprights the centre gave Buckland a chance to exhibit his capabilities as a "shootist," but Harry's shot was a trifle inaccurate and hit the outside of the net. Still keeping up the pressure, Rowlands essayed a capital centre, which Hutcheson received, and on transferring to Hibbard, that player shot, but was penalised for an infringement of the off-side rule. From the free-kick Swindon could not make any headway, Tyler affording Rowlands and Buckland a chance of again becoming aggressive, the former forcing a corner off Vowles, from which no tangible advantage accrued. Ashdown made a bad miss in close proximity to goal and let in the right wing. A scramble ensued in front of Taylor's domains, but ultimately Auld came to the assistance of his side and transferred the ball into safer territory. Jenner obtained possession and as he was careering down the field he was fouled by Spackman, the free kick being of no use to Brompton, as Richardson cleared, and enabled Mahoney to take a shot, which went high over the bar. Considering the elements the New Brompton men were playing remarkably well, the defence in particular, and were never caught napping. Four corners fell to Swindon, but the visitors failed to improve upon them. Rowlands at the other end got in a fine centre, but the centre and right wing were not up to receive it, and the ball rolled over the line. New Brompton had to defend again, and were successful in keeping their goal intact up till half-time, the score being—

Swindon Town .... 1 goal
New Brompton .... love.

THE "COLONIALS" TOP ON TWO POINTS IN THE SECOND HALF.

With the aid of such a boisterous wind, victory stared the "Colonials" in the face, especially as the visitors were only leading by a goal. Buckland was the first to try and lower Williams' colours, but his attempt sailed round into touch, just passing the upright. Hibbard, Hutcheson, and Buckland were causing no little trouble to Vowles and Richardson, who were in for a lively time, and after Hibbard had missed an opportunity Hutcheson secured and "let fly," but Richardson put in an appearance and booted the ball away. New Brompton did not let the Swindon men have any rest, and it seemed certain that they would score. The ball seemed to be going into touch, and would have gone had it not been for Hibbard, who rushed past Vowles and brought the ball in front of the goal with the back of his head. A scrimmage ensued, but burly Williams came out with flying colours and cleared his charge, a feat he performed on four other occasions in quick succession. The right wing of the Swindon team transferred the play by means of good passing to the other end, but the Brompton defence was on the alert and Auld sent them back again. New Brompton scored their first goal directly after this. Hutcheson got possession, and made a capital position for Jenner. The speedy rightwinger took full advantage of his opportunity, and rushed forward and landed the ball safely past Williams, hitting the top of the net in its flight. This achievement was received with vociferous cheering, whilst some thought that Jenner was suspiciously off-side, an opinion which held good on account of his passing the two backs. Encouraged by this success, the Brompton men forced the play. Some fine neat passing by the right wing and the centre followed, the run being ended by a splendid cross-shot by Hutcheson. Williams stopped another raid by the Bromptonians in a very clever manner. Swindon were successful in getting away on two or three occasions, but were very rarely dangerous. Parker was penalised for fouling Buckland, but from the free kick Hibbard landed the ball high over, and hands against Rowlands and Tyler respectively afforded them very little relief. Rowlands was the next to show up and he essayed a fine shot, which only missed by inches. It was thought that the ball on one occasion had passed into the goal. Jenner planted the ball nicely to Buckland, and the latter with great promptitude tried a shot. Williams, who was hampered by Jenner, saved in the corner of the goal, but it was a very near thing. Andrews, for Swindon, was conspicuous for a nice run, but James deprived him. Soon afterwards the Swindon goal had another narrow squeak from a free kick for hands, the sphere being cleared after an exciting scrimmage. The aggressive work was mainly done by Brompton, and the forwards were showing very fair combination, whilst the half-backs were very prominent, James doing some wonderfully neat work. Hands against Mahoney was of no benefit to Brompton, as Hayward got possession and started off for the other end, but after baffling Liddle, his progress was checked by Auld. Hibbard deserved to score (on receiving from Jenner) with a beautiful long shot passing just over the bar. A persistent attack on the visitors' citadel ended in a corner being forced. Hibbard undertook the kick, and put the ball well out, allowing for the wind. James got possession and lifted the ball over his head, and it dropped immediately in front of the uprights, where another scrimmage took place, but the Swindon defenders were not so lucky on this occasion in effecting a clearance, as Jenner, whilst lying on the ground, managed to scoop the ball past Williams, thus giving the Bromptonians the lead, amid loud cheering. On the restart the Swindon men tried to draw level. Reynolds immediately taking the ball up the ground, but Ashdown forced him to kick into touch. Then Hibbard gave Williams a teaser to contend with in the form of a swift ground shot, and he kicked it away, the ball hitting Hutcheson and rebounding into touch. Nothing more of any interest occurred, and New Brompton were left victorious by a nose too interesting game by the narrow margin of a goal.

New Brompton .... 2 goals
Swindon Town .... 1 goal.

Outside the Medway however momentous decisions were being made regarding professionalism, which was practically unknown in the South of England, and also the formation of a new league known as the Southern League. This arose out of a dispute between Millwall and Everton regarding the former's need to pay the latter £100 because of the purchase of two Scottish players who, although they had signed a contract with Everton, had never in fact seen the ground let alone played for the team. The dispute led to boycotts of friendly games which in turn led to the Southern Clubs having a decimated fixture list. To counteract the boycott the Southern League was formed in January.

Within a short time the Directors of New Brompton knew that they had to be part of the League if they were to keep quality football in the Medway area and accordingly on the 11th May called a meeting at the 'Napier Arms'. A Newspaper report of the time explains: "The Directors, who are anxious that professionalism should exist, put forward two schemes for the consideration of the players, but after a lively and long discussion they were rejected. Afterwards, the players were requested to suggest a plan, which would be agreeable to themselves, which they did, and the Directors, taking into full consideration, decided to accept it. Then came the important business of getting the players to promise to sign professional forms, but as matters turned out, this part of the proceedings was easily manipulated, and amongst those who consented were Hutcheson (Captain), who gave his name first, Auld, Jenner, Ashdown, Buckland, whilst the Directors are sure of James and Liddle affixing their signatures when the time for so doing arrives. The Directors do not mean to pay exorbitant sums to players, but by the method laid down, the expenses incurred would amount to about £1 per man per match. Dickinson the ex Bolton Wanderer, would play for Brompton next season as an amateur, whilst one or two other prominent players might be seen in their ranks".

Immediately on joining the Southern League Division II they played twelve matches and won eleven, scoring 57 goals and conceding 10. Promotion was, however, not automatic in those days and it was necessary for test matches to take place. Scoring five goals in such a match against Swindon gave the 'Black and Whites' entry into the First Division.

But by far and away the most important matter on the Directorate's plate was that of finance. The early Minutes of the Company show that the ground was used for sheep grazing, athletics and fetes all of which assisted the ever decreasing coffers.

Although it is difficult to ascertain exactly what a trainer did in 1894 the Club decided to get one. Managers as such did not exist nor did tactics. Eleven men would go out on the pitch in a 2-8 formation and kick the ball in a certain direction for 45 minutes and in the opposite direction for a further 45 minutes. But though there may have been a certain lack of discipline on the pitch the Directors were certainly not going to allow it to spread to the dressing room. Something, although exactly what we shall never know, was going slightly awry with the new club and this was rectified in August 1894 when one of the players was summoned before the Directorate to "vindicate or otherwise his character". In addition it was agreed that there would now be two practices every week; all complaints from players to be brought forward by the Captain and that there should be proper accounts kept of practices and training. Further, "the dressing rooms be entered by nobody with the exception of the Directors and those men on duty". Finally a Mr. Mercer was charged threepence for damaging the goal net!

1895 is the first occasion where a team selection is minuted. On the 4th January the following were chosen to play for New Brompton at Gravesend — Russell — Auld, Ashdown — James, Pellat, Meager — Thomas, Hutcheson, Jenner, Buckland and Dickinson. Interestingly this shows the classic 2-3-5 formation. It so happens that Jenner didn't play having received an injury in the Dockyard and Webb, a reserve, played in his place.

Things must have been getting rather rough for our band of licensed victuallers and others at this stage as the groundsman was interviewed and in view of the financial position of the Company was given one week's notice of dismissal. Notwithstanding this he still played in goal the next week! At the same time it was debated by the Directors "That the first team players be called together and asked to take a reduction in appearance money", but this motion was lost and the

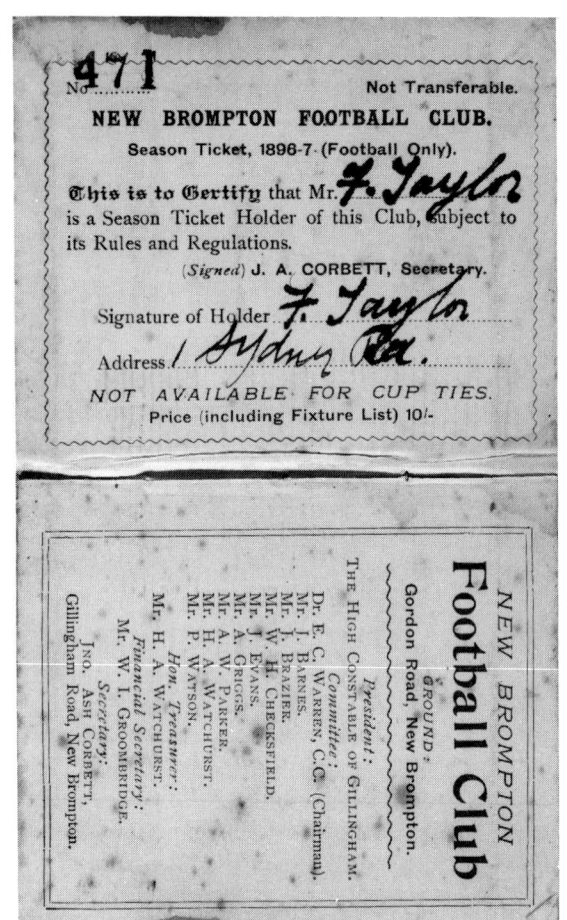
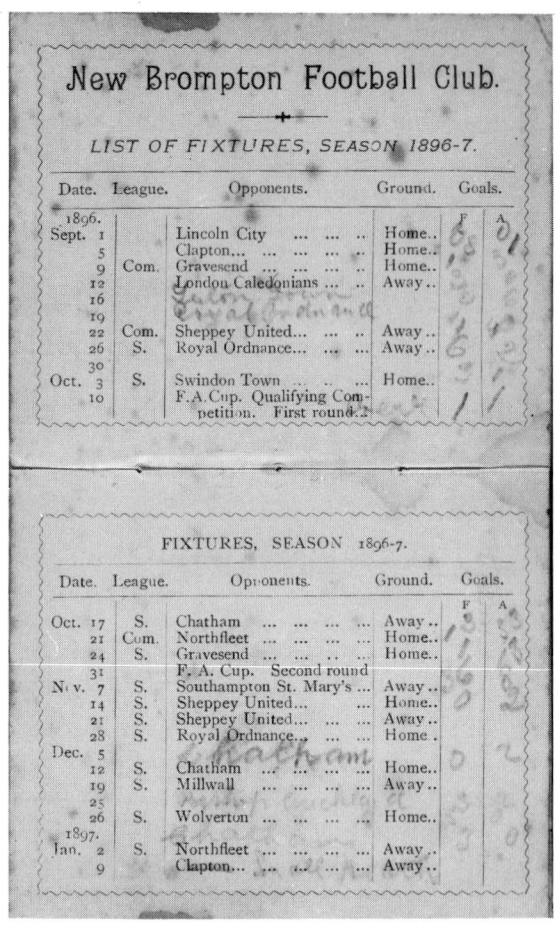
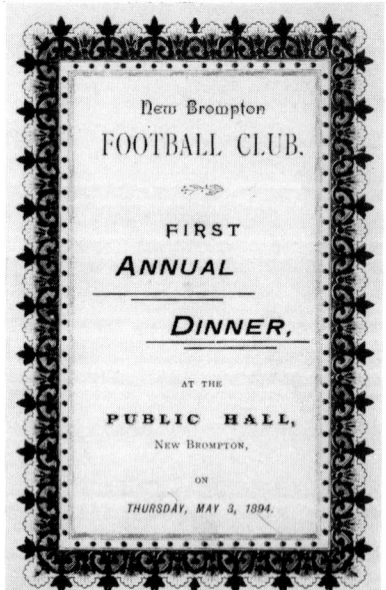
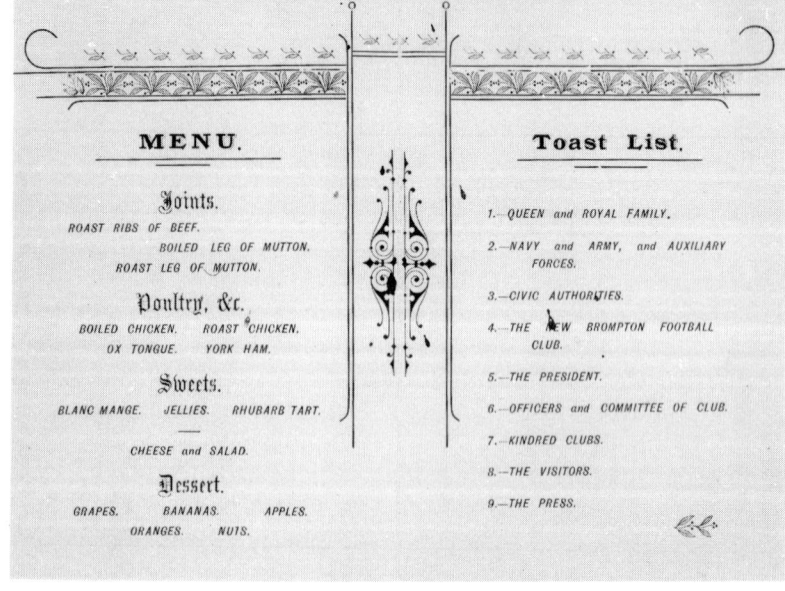

... even the Press were toasted!

New Brompton F.C., League Team
Winners of the Chatham and Rochester Charity Cup 1895-6
Mr J. Evans, Mr A.W. Partridge, Mr J. Barnes, Mr P. Watson, Mr W.H. Checksfield
W.J. Murray (Trainer), Mr H.A. Watchurst (Hon Treas), F. Manning, D. Hutcheson, J.W. Gascoine, A. Meager,
Mr H. Clother (Secretary)
Dr E.C. Warren (Chairman), W.E. Thomas, H. Buckland, D. Pellatt (Captain), F. McNamee, D. Bruce, Mr A.W. Parker
P. Cochran, P. Gladwell, J. Walker, J. Cockrill

matter was not raised with the players. In February of 1895 a deputation went to see the Bank Manager and this was to be the first of a long line of such deputations over the following year. During this particular financial crisis there may well have been a football strike at the ground for the Minutes show that the 'A' team appeared before the Board and a Mr. Drew, who acted as their spokesman, stated that they had 'acted hastily in refusing to play Chatham B on account of unfair treatment by the Directorate'. When researching one can often be frustrated. This incident, if more were known, could well be of historic significance, possibly Nationally, as the first (and only?) football strike.

With the Inland Revenue pressing, in March a debate, perhaps of some violence, occurred between the Directors as to whether they would be prepared to allow a Ladies Football Club to play on the ground to help the funds. One suggested that it "should not be entertained", however his views did not prevail and to the enjoyment of the populace, Gillingham Young Ladies frolicked on the pitch so earning the club £79.12s.4½d. Ironically a couple of weeks beforehand New Brompton had played a local derby and had earned only £7 more. As to whether the Victorians watched the Ladies for their football skills or for other reasons can only be guessed at. Sadly no photographs are available.

New Brompton Football Club 1902-3
E. Killean, E. Daw, A. Archer
H.A. Watchurst (Hon Treas), W. McCurdy, W. Raisbeck, H. Goldie, J. Elliott, J. Lofthouse (Trainer),
W.I. Groombridge (Sec)
J.J. Bradbury, G. Smith, A. Milward, C.O. Satterthwaite, A.E. Dunkley
T. Leigh

New Brompton Football Club 1904-5
Mr J.G. Groombridge (Sec), Craddock (Trainer), Watts, Mr G. Barnes, Griffiths, Mr G. Swayn
Elliott, Mckie, Boucher, Turner, Lager, White
Barnfather, Leigh, Morris

Chapter 3

New Brompton had won the Southern League Division II (1894/5), the Chatham and District Charity Cup (1893/4) (1895/6) and were finalists in 1899 and 1900. They had also won the Thames and Medway Combination Championship Cup on two occasions. The Club must have been optimistic at the dawn of the 20th Century; it had a few years under its belt and even though financially it may not have been a great success it was proving an effective force on the field, finishing high in the League each season.

By the beginning of the 1900's the game of football had crystallised. Now there were goal posts and nets, as opposed to a tape hung above two pieces of wood; distinct rules had been formulated and the game received the patronage of none other than the Prince of Wales when he first attended a game in March 1886, visiting Kennington Oval for a charity festival which included a soccer match between the 'Gentlemen' and the 'Players'. His interest encouraged others and with the minor irritants in the game such as how to take a throw-in (two hands first introduced in 1882) and exactly how many players should play on each side being sorted out, football had become a recognised sport.

One set of games in the season 1899/1900 stand out and they relate to the Football Association Cup. New Brompton were drawn against Woolwich Arsenal. It was the third qualifying round and playing away in Southampton, New Brompton still known as 'The Colonists' drew 1-1. The re-play in Medway ended in another draw so that a third meeting was necessary; playing at Millwall both teams scored twice and a fourth game, this time at Tottenham, ended in yet another draw of 1-1. The fifth match turned out to be a decider when at Gravesend, New Brompton were victorious 1-0. In the next round (the fourth) they were drawn against Thames Ironworks (an insignificant East London Club who sported a crossed hammers badge) at home, drew, only to lose the re-play at Canning Town, 2-0.

At the end of 1901 New Brompton finished eleventh and subsequent seasons saw them tenth, sixth and in sixteenth positions. But what is particularly interesting is to compare the Club Secretary, Mr Groombridge's statement "The Directors have each year had a hard uphill fight, but population, support, and enthusiasm grow each season, and before many years New Brompton should rank as one of the strongest clubs in the Southern League", with the reality of the situation as shown from the Minute Books.

Even with the increase in the population of Gillingham (which went from twenty one thousand to forty two thousand, in ten years) financial matters were still uppermost in the minds of the Directors. The gates were just not good enough and on the 25th, April 1902, so as to extricate themselves from an extremely embarrassing financial situation the club transferred part of the land it owned for £2,500. Today this is Gordon Road. At about the same time the Directors made a public statement that "In their endeavours to continue providing class football the Directors regret that they have not yet received sufficient public support to make it remunerative. In the playing field the Company's team had a fairly satisfactory course. At home they were invincible against the leading Southern League Clubs. Portsmouth, Tottenham. . . all failing to score".

But our friends were not ones to allow economic gloom to overshadow their moral responsibility, and whilst selling the land passed a resolution condemning "boys playing cards on the football ground on Sundays".

Such was the like of football Directors in the 'jingoistic' and exciting earlier part of the 1900's; the Empire continued to expand, troop movements in Chatham, which had been a large base since the early 1800's supplied supporters and players alike. The free-for-all age had also affected the players who began pressing a little harder for higher salaries. Intensive negotiations no doubt took place in the case of T. Leigh who on 21st April, 1902 stated he "would not accept the terms offered by the Board but would accept £1.15s. per week summer and £2.10s. per week playing season". The Board agreed but would not give "Mr Harris (goalkeeper) nor Mr Killean (Back) £2 summer and £3 playing season which they had asked for." At the same time the Club is beginning to look further afield for players chasing a "Mr. W. Orr (Back) of Manchester City and W. Raisbeck (Half-back) of Derby County" — continual references are now made to £10 bonuses which are to be paid on signings.

In some ways, however, players had not changed for in November 1903 Davidson was "Again called before the Directors and admitted fighting with Bradbury on two occasions on Saturday evening last. After hearing the evidence of several witnesses it was resolved to suspend Davidson and fine Bradbury £1." Then Stevenson was fined five shillings for attending late and being 'the worse for drink', and Goldie 'severely censured for arriving late'. To attempt to enforce discipline it was resolved that in future the trainer should close the training book ten minutes after the time that players were warned to attend the ground. Such warnings as were given did not seem to work as within a few days Goldie and Boucher arrived for training the worse for drink. Fines and suspensions followed but so did the consumption of alcohol and throughout the Minute Book for some years complaints are being made by Directors, Trainers and so on about players being 'tipsy'. Some may find it paradoxical that the Directors, who made their living from alcohol should censure those who drank it, but then again it is not our job to view the morals of our fore-fathers.

Within ten years of having sold the excess ground the Club's overdraft at the London and Provincial Bank had begun to creep to an unacceptable level. Though the team had finished seventh in 1908/9 with a score of forty eight goals (their highest since promotion to the Southern League Division One), the crowds had not been there. November 1911 showed the overdraft at £693 with Tottenham Hotspur insisting on £500 for the transfer of Wilkes. To enable a club of quality to exist support was necessary and there was a genuine threat to wind up the Company in 1912 unless the gates grew substantially. At the time of collecting £20.13s. during a match for the 'Titanic Fund' the Club was in an embarrassing position concerning paying players' wages; £150 per gate was required to keep the Club afloat and in order to continue for the remainder of the season 1912/13 it was found necessary to raise a second mortgage and thus enable the Directors to clear the Bank overdraft, pay the players wages (which had been deferred) and settle necessary debts. There was talk of a supporters club which it was hoped would assist in obtaining urgent finance. Ideas of all sorts were mooted and some accepted; the turnstiles were loaned to Gillingham Council for a small fee and a sandwich board was allowed to be walked around the ground during an F.A. Cup Tie for £4, smoking concerts were held, as were fetes.

When looking at Gillingham's past the whole of one's work could be an examination of the economic struggles through the years. This would be unfair as football was, believe it or not, still being played at Priestfield Stadium during these times! Yet I feel drawn to the personalities of the Directors and Players, hundreds of the latter who will never be known to us and who struggled to enable a football club to survive.

Chapter 4

By 1913 Gillingham, originally a small suburb of Brompton, had become larger than its 'Mother' — In step with the times an extraordinary general meeting was held at the 'Napier Arms' on the 17th July 1913 where it was resolved that the name of the Company be changed from The New Brompton Football Club Limited to the Gillingham Football Club Company Limited and this was confirmed at a further meeting held on the 7th August 1913.

That season, Gillingham entered its twenty first year and this proved to be its most successful to date. Increased crowds and good results meant that the Directors were in a position to clear outstanding accounts and on the 18th June 1914, the thought of a new stand arose. It was agreed that this be built for about £1,400. One can, retrospectively, see the gladdened faces of the Directors at that meeting considering, perhaps, a new era occurring for their club, a new stand, greater comfort for the spectators and bigger gates. It all looked promising. Little did they know that shortly after their decision the Archduke Ferdinand of Austria and his Wife would be assassinated, lighting the powder trail to the First World War which was declared by Britain on Germany on the 4th August, 1914.

In October of that year the Club like every other must have been experiencing problems, to say the least, but we see it taking its part in the Community War effort by allowing the ground to be used to collect money for the Mayor's Belgian Relief Fund and that of the Prince of Wales; recruits were allowed to play for charity and so forth. Conversely their charity did not extend to their players as far as a Mr Glen was concerned. He asked the Directors for permission to marry on Christmas Day 1914 but this was refused, "it being resolved by the Board that he be requested to arrange for his Wedding to take place on the Monday" instead. With the influx of men into the forces a player was beginning to become valuable property!

But with quality players moving into the Army, salaries did not increase and due to the low gates in December of the first year of the War players were asked to accept a reduction of twenty five per cent in their salaries. Even so the year ending May 1915 showed heavy losses which were wholly attributable to the "unparallel conditions prevailing throughout the Country caused through the unfortunate War". There existed a Footballers' Battalion and arrangements had been made with the Army for players to have leave on Saturdays. However the problem really was the lack of spectators.

The years 1914/1919 were bleak for the World and Gillingham Football Club did not escape the reverberations of the 'War to end all Wars'. As the demands of the Army grew so there were fewer players and spectators. Many clubs throughout the country closed their gates as villages and towns became decimated of men and boys. Gillingham staggered on arranging local friendlies with the help of the soldiers, but all in all this is a depressing period. If it had not been for the support of the troops, many of whom were naturally stationed in Chatham and "who much appreciated the few hours' recreation" the clubs could not have continued.

The majority of people in England had no reason to know that the twenties were 'naughty'. They went to football matches to escape from 'the dark of despondency into the light of combat. . . to win was personal success, to lose another clout from life. From these shared values arose a particular culture of football. Support containing specific ways of watching and participating in football passed on through families, neighbours and friends to each new generation'.

War having drawn to an end it was anticipated that a new tomorrow would begin but this was certainly not the case for the 'Gills'. As the soldiers returned home Gillingham were re-elected to the Southern League along with Swansea Town, Brentford and Merthyr and at the same time

She:— "Candidly, I don't think much of that one. I hope the next will be better!"

agreed to change their colours back to the former black and white stripe which was to remain for another twelve years.

The season 1919/20 was disastrous, the team conceding 74 goals and scoring a mere 34. But to perhaps balance this funds in plenty arrived as a population bereft of public entertainment for over four years, rushed to enjoy the pleasures of football again.

No doubt because of the results on the pitch the Manager resigned and after an interview with Mr. J. McMillan of Whitecross Street, Derby the Directors resolved that he should be appointed as the new Manager at a salary of seven pounds per week and that as an addition he would be allowed bonuses for wins and draws as allowed by the League. Just after this J. J. Kennedy was appointed the club's trainer at five pounds per week. Signings were made to solidify the team which had up to forty players, off and on, in the previous season.

At the Football League's Annual General Meeting it was agreed that clubs which formed the Southern League, Division I, would be elected to comprise the new Football League Division III for the season 1920/21 and accordingly on the 28th August, 1920, Gillingham found themselves playing their first match in Division III, a game with Southampton which they drew 1-1. Sadly the form of the Club did not pick up for some time and as month followed month the situation became worse. Yet even so at the end of May, 1921, the receipts were over £13,000 and this exceeded all previous records, the Club was watched by 200,000 people which "proved that football is a very popular sport in the Borough and District".

The late Mrs Battiste, wife of Wally who played as a right winger, told me shortly before her death this year "I remember the ground well in those days. We sat on benches and the ground had a little hedge around it, no fence or anything like that, just a hedge where the kids collected. And it was such a friendly Club. When we arrived from Grimsby we were lost, arriving at Chatham Station instead of Gillingham. We didn't know the buses or anything. Eventually we were met by Ginger Simmonds and he was so helpful and nice, taking us to our digs in Toronto Road. It was

Gillingham F.C. 1920-21
Robertson, Battiste, Baxter, Wigmore, Sissons, Needham
McMillan (Manager), Holt, Hall, Branfield, Gilby, Rowe, Gore, Kennedy (Trainer)

a family Club in those days, all the players and staff mixed together socially and were friends. And Mr Curtis, the Manager, was a real Gentleman."

Unable to break out of mediocre form during 1921/22 the clouds began their regular gathering. At a meeting held on the 3rd May 1923 with £3,000 now owing at the Bank there were suggestions that the Club be closed down, but it was proposed by Councillors Neil and Phillips "that in the opinion of this meeting further effort be made to continue the Club." This was carried unanimously, a public meeting was arranged and a committee set up at once to start the struggle.

And struggle it was. Rochester Bill Posting Co. agreed to wait a little longer for payment of a £15.00 bill, but the local Newsagents sent a Solicitor's letter demanding payment within 14 days of the 'long outstanding account of £49.1s.6d.' There were others who pressed for their accounts to be settled and all were held off by the Directors for as long as possible.

By 1923, with unemployment causing acute distress, it was suggested that those registered as unemployed should be allowed in at half price so as to help the gates. This was rejected for practical reasons, and at around that time, perhaps feeling his age, The Secretary, Groombridge, who had been involved with the Club for nearly thirty years, decided that he wished to resign his position.

FIXTURES, SEASON 1920-21.

THE FOOTBALL LEAGUE.
Third Division. Southern Section.

Date.		Ground.	For	Against
Aug. 28	Southampton	Home		
Sept. 1	Reading	Away		
" 4	Southampton	Away		
" 8	Reading	Home		
" 11	Merthyr Town	Home		
" 15	Portsmouth	Home		
" 18	Merthyr Town	Away		
" 25	Plymouth Argyle	Away		
Oct. 2	Plymouth Argyle	Home		
" 9	Exeter City	Away		
" 16	Exeter City	Home		
" 23	Millwall	Away		
" 30	Millwall	Home		
Nov. 6	Newport County	Away		
" 13	Newport County	Home		
" 20	E.C.	Away		
" 27	Portsmouth	Away		
Dec. 4	Swindon Town	Home		
" 11	Swindon Town	Away		
" 18	Watford	Home		
" 25	Northampton	Home		
" 27	Northampton	Away		
" 28	Luton Town	Away		
1921.				
Jan. 1	Watford	Away		
" 8	E.C. First Round			
" 15	Brentford	Home		
" 22	Brentford	Away		
" 29	Bristol Rovers	Home		
Feb. 5	Bristol Rovers	Away		
" 12	Norwich City	Home		
" 19	Norwich City	Away		
" 26	Crystal Palace	Away		
Mar. 5	Crystal Palace	Home		
" 12	Brighton and Hove	Home		
" 19	Brighton and Hove	Away		
" 25	Southend	Away		
" 28	Southend United	Away		
Apl. 2	Grimsby Town	Home		
" 9	Queen's Park Rangers	Away		
" 16	Queen's Park Rangers	Home		
" 23	Swansea Town	Away		
" 30	Swansea Town	Home		
May 7	Luton Town	Home		

SOUTHERN LEAGUE.

Date.		Ground.	For	Against
Aug. 28	Reading	Away		
Sept. 4	Reading	Home		
" 18	Clapton Orient	Home		
" 25	Boscombe	Home		
Oct. 2	Southampton	Home		
" 16	Boscombe	Away		
" 23		Home		
" 30	Southampton	Away		
Nov. 6	Millwall	Home		
" 13	Chatham	Away		
" 20	Portsmouth	Away		
" 27	Portsmouth	Home		
Dec. 11	West Ham	Home		
" 18	Watford	Away		
" 27		Home		
1921.				
Jan. 1	Watford	Home		
" 15	Thornycrofts	Away		
" 22	Crystal Palace	Home		
" 29	Millwall	Away		
Feb. 5	Chatham	Home		
" 12	Norwich City	Away		
" 19	Norwich City	Home		
Mar. 5	Thornycrofts	Home		
" 12	Brighton and Hove	Away		
" 19	Brighton and Hove	Home		
" 26	Luton Town	Home		
" 28		Home		
Apl. 2	Charlton	Away		
" 9	Charlton	Home		
" 23		Home		
" 30	Crystal Palace	Away		
May 7	Luton Town	Away		

SEASON TICKETS £2/10/0 (including tax) Reserved and Numbered, Centre New Stand and First Two Rows Gordon Road Stand. £2/2/0 (including tax) Unreserved.

The Swiss Cafe and Restaurant
(F. FERRARI & SON, PROPRIETORS)

FIRST-CLASS MENUS A LA CARTE & TABLE D' HÔTE

Efficient Service. Civility and Cleanliness. Parties catered for.

6c, High Street, Gillingham.
(OPPOSITE "THE CRICKETERS")

W. & J. Mackay & Co., Ltd., 54, High Street, Gillingham.

Gillingham Football Club Co., LTD.

OFFICIAL PROGRAMME & LIST OF FIXTURES
Season 1920-21. Football League & Southern League.
PRICE 1d.

C. E. BOUGHTON
Dental Surgery,
64, Canterbury Street, Gillingham.

PAINLESS EXTRACTIONS.
Artificial Teeth—Fit Guaranteed.
Fillings, Gold Crowns and Bridge Work.
Teeth Cleaned.
Repairs (any make) finished in a few hours.
Children's Teeth attended to.
Terms arranged.

NOTE ADDRESS—
64, CANTERBURY STREET, GILLINGHAM, KENT.

Gillingham Football Club Co., Ltd.

Saturday, 11th Sept., 1920. Kick off 3.30 p.m.

THE FOOTBALL LEAGUE. Third Division.
Southern Section.

Gillingham v. Merthyr Town.

GILLINGHAM TEAM.

Goal
Branfield

Right Back: **Robertson**   Left Back: **Shaw**

Right Half: **Battiste**   Centre Half: **Thompson**   Left Half: **Wigmore**

Outside Right: **Holt**   Inside Right: **Hall**   Centre: **Gilbey**   Inside Left: **Roe**   Outside Left: **Gore**

Linesmen—Mr. T. W. CURTIS (Southend), Mr. S. H. COOPER (London).

Outside Left: **Edwards**   Inside Left: **Chisser**   Centre: **Walker**   Inside Right: **Nicholas**   Outside Right: **William**

Left Half: **Crowe**   Centre Half: **Jennings**   Right Half: **Byron**

Left Back: **Clarke**   Right Back: **Copeland**

Goal
Lindon

MERTHYR TOWN TEAM.

Next Home Matches
Wednesday, 15th September, v. PORTSMOUTH (Football League). Kick off 5.45 p.m.
Saturday, 18th September, v. CLAPTON ORIENT. Kick off 3.30 p.m.

SPECIAL TRAIN leaves Strood 2.45 every Saturday match during September and October, returning 5.23 and 5.45. Wednesday, 15th v. Portsmouth, from Strood 5.20, returning 7.47.

List of Players. Season 1920-21.

	Name.	Age.	Height Ft. In.	Weight St. Lbs.	Club played for
Goal	J. Branfield	27	5 9	10 8	Gillingham
	E. Ollerenshaw				Manchester City
	R. Lee	24	5 10	11 0	Gillingham
	T. W. Read	22	5 9½	11 2	Royal Navy
Backs	A. Milton	24	5 9	12 0	Coventry
	Thos. Baxter	27	5 10	11 8	Chelsea (Bk. or Half)
	Thos. Sissons	21	5 8½	11 2	Hucknell Byron
	J. W. Robertson	23	5 10	11 2	Gillingham
	C. E. Shaw	21	5 8	11 0	Rosington
Half Backs	W. Battiste	25	5 8	11 0	Grimsby (Right Half or Forward)
	C. Wigmore	26	5 9	11 0½	Aston Villa (Left Half)
	T. N. Thompson	26	5 9	11 12	Sunderland (Centre Half)
	J. W. Needham	21		11 0	Derby (Centre Forward or Half)
	H. L. Rowden	21	5 9½	11 0	Chatham Central (Centre Half)
	F. L. Combs				Sheppy (Half Back)
	J. A. Giffiths				Gillingham (Half Back)
Forwards	A. Holt	25	5 8	11 0	Chesterfield (Outside Right)
	C. Cradock	18	5 9	10 0	Chatham Central (Outside Right)
	D. McCormick	21	5 9	10 7	Gillingham (Inside Forward)
	T. E. Gilby	22	5 9	11 0½	Darlington (Centre or Inside)
	T. Hall	28	5 8	11 0	Newcastle (Centre or Inside)
	A. Roe	25	5 8	11 0½	Birmingham (Centre or Inside)
	A. B. Wood	20	5 9	11 0	Gillingham (Centre or Inside)
	F. J. Howard	24	5 9	11 0	Derby (Inside Forward)
	C. Hancock	26	5 9	10 10	Goole (Outside Left)
	T. J. D. Robinson	28	5 9	11 0½	Everton (Inside Forward)
	A. J. Carter	24	5 8	10 8	Zion (Outside Left)
	S. P. Gore				Faversham (Outside Left)

The team of 1923/24 with Directors and local Dignitaries. Team: Read, Robertson, Thompson, Hendrie, Needham, North, Curtis (Manager), Battiste, Cosgrove, Fox, Hall, Sinning, Kane (Trainer).

In early 1924, the Gills sensationalised the Football Association Cup by holding Cardiff City, who were then a classic side, to a goal-less draw at Ninian Park. The re-play brought 20,000 spectators to the ground with receipts of over £1,000; sadly Gillingham lost. It can be imagined, however, the atmosphere which pervaded the club with such a large gate. Shortly after Gillingham had the honour of their player Freddie Fox being selected to play for England against France.

One record was achieved during the twenties and that was the nine and a half hour cup games against Barrow where thousands saw the teams draw and draw again, Barrow eventually picking up the honours by beating the Gills 2-1. This record stood for thirty years.

To merely talk about football in relation to a football club is not telling the whole story. I tried earlier to give an indication of the involvement which a town and its people has with a club. In January 1926, to enable the game against Bristol Rovers to take place it was necessary to employ a number of men to clear the snow from the pitch. Voluntary helpers appeared with horses and worked non-stop to prepare the ground for the game. It was only three quarters of an hour before the kick-off that the work was completed. Compensation for this work was recorded in the Gills winning by six goals to three in a game where they totally outplayed the visitors. Was it by any chance this personalised relationship between the supporters and the team which urged the latter on to such heights or merely luck? In the same month the club sold Edmead to

Gillingham F.C. 1932-33
A. Ure, A. Forbes, F. Maven, R. Jackson, R. Bethell, T. Holland,
A. Collins, G. Kidd, F. Lester, C. Gelatley, Mr Crumbie
W. Armfield, G. Purcell, J. Nichol, S. Raleigh, F. Liddle

Liverpool for £1,700 which, although causing distress to the fans, placated the Bank Manager.

1928/29 turned out to be an extremely dismal year when Gillingham had again to apply for re-election finishing at the bottom of the table and they repeated this the year afterwards. A study of the twenties is disappointing from one angle if one takes the view that the only thing worth writing about is success. Managers and financial problems continued but so did the loyal support, or should I say the passion for Kent's foremost football team. Supporters' committees continued through the hard times fighting to acquire finance for the club's assistance, and to maintain first-class football in the District. Various schemes were organised such as whist drives and dances, Sunday concerts, boxing tournaments, Christmas draw, Stop Watch competitions (?) holiday draws and boat trips; donations were obtained from pubs, restaurants, businesses; and advertising was arranged, all of which linked the team even tighter with the community which surrounded it and to which it acted as a beacon of light in a particularly depressed society. One can envisage the complex and erudite debates which occurred on the terraces in say September, 1930, concerning the F.A. Law Number 17. This stated that when a penalty kick was to be taken 'the opponents goalkeeper must stand on his own goal line until the ball is kicked'. The word 'stand' had to be defined after alleged infringements by 'keepers and the exact definition was decided by the F.A. as 'must not move his feet'. And then again it may be of interest to note that the F.A. issued a notice (published fully in the Gills programme) as a result of one or two problems which were occurring during games. It stated that players 'must not question a referee's decision, but accept it without demur. To approach or argue with a referee, to touch him or show dissent is ungentlemanly behaviour...'

The thirties were supposed to have style. This was not mirrored in Gillingham's play and the new era meant an immediate application for re-election. In January 1932, a fresh Manager, Fred Maven, was appointed and in his first season 1932/33 the team dragged itself from the bottom half of the division finishing respectably above half way, the centre forward Nicol scoring some twenty-four league goals. There was some discussion going on at the time by the league concerning the possible experiment of numbering of players.

On the 1st December, 1934, the team lined up against Brighton and Hove, the centre forward being Sid Raleigh. It was just another game, Gillingham lying fifth from the bottom of the Third Division (South) with Brighton fourth from the top. Tragically Sid was concussed during the match as a result of the collision with, it would seem, Mooney, the Brighton centre half. Sid, the ex-miner, died that night in St. Bartholomew's Hospital with his wife beside him.

The thirties proved to be years of consistent decline which reached their nadir in 1938. An average crowd in the region of 10,000 was turning up regularly to see a team in the doldrums; defeat followed defeat with new ideas failing and players being sold. Eventually at the end of the season, notwithstanding the efforts of Herbert, Watson and Wilson (who together scored over half of Gillingham's goals in that season) the team found itself with the wooden spoon, Millwall winning the league, closely challenged by Queens Park Rangers.

It seemed a formality the club would be re-elected. However, the young Ipswich Town polled thirty six votes and Walsall thirty four. Gillingham obtained only twenty eight and thus the Medway Towns were without league football. Having only scored thirty-six goals that season, small crowds (compared with Ipswich and Walsall) and the fact that this was their fifth application for re-election, naturally went against them.

The catastrophe at Priestfield Road was soon to be overtaken as the World went to war again.

CHATHAM OBSERVER, NOVEMBER 28th, 1947

Chapter 5

As Dr. Grossmark once said "The story of Gillingham Football Club covers periods of purple, grey and black" and as you cannot get blacker than black things just had to get better — hadn't they?

A study of the Club during the War years up until total demobilisation of the troops is difficult if not impossible; matches were arranged ad hoc with players chosen from other teams by both sides. The idea was to keep the glimmer of football alive during these difficult years to provide some form of entertainment, when possible, for a Nation desperately desiring it.

Power and vitality burst on the Priestfield Stadium during the mid-forties and this is perhaps one of the best periods since inception. In 1944/45 the team won the Kent League, and in the next year repeated the performance, scoring a devastating one hundred and eleven goals and conceding thirty-three. Winning eighteen of their twenty games they must have appeared like a modern Liverpool to the opposition. With the League title plus the Kent Senior Cup and Kent Senior Shield to their credit, they had made Club and County history by winning everything Kent football had to offer. Entering the Southern League the next season they were to win that as well!

At the start of the 1946 season quality football was being played at Gillingham and paraphrasing W. S. Churchill, the Vice Chairman W. S. Cox gave the cry "Give us the gates and we will deliver the goods."

The undoubted driving force behind the success was Archie Clark who had joined the Club at the beginning of the War but could not really start to build a team until its finalisation. In a period of time when the call-up was effective and when it was not always as simple as it sounds to obtain players who were doing their National Service, Clark put together a team of outstanding ability, and in 1946 occurred one of the great moments in football history. It was the 9th November and Gillingham lay fifth in the Southern League with Gloucester City fourth from the bottom. On that day Stuart Wilson netted nine of his club's twelve goals. Five were scored before half time and at the end of the match Gloucester City joined in the crowds' tribute.

These were the boom years of football, for five years people had had little or no entertainment and now they flocked to the ground. Six hundred travelled to see the team beat Guildford 2-1 on the 16th November. The newspaper report of the time quotes "The little Club which used to be the cinderella of football is stirring lustily in a bid to enter the League again. This new Gillingham is averaging gates of 8,000 and nine big-time Managers watched a recent mid-week game."

Although being quoted at 1,000-1 to win the Cup (Arsenal were 50-1) they knocked out Bristol City at Bristol, by two goals to one, the scorers being Russell and Wilson. And in January 1947 once again the volunteers poured in to clear the pitch of snow in an effort to have the ground ready for playing.

Oh, what superb days these were for the fans! In March '47 Gillingham were top of the Southern League having played twenty games and gained thirty-two points. There was excitement as well. Against Bury Town, although six nil up at half time, the Gills were forced to concede six in the second half and the score finished level. I have strong feeling that with twelve goals being seen everybody went home satisfied.

In their last game of the season against Bedford in what must have been one of the most exciting games ever played at the Stadium, before 8,000 spectators in the pouring rain they put six goals past their opponents and finished runners-up in the Southern League. They had won the Kent Senior Cup and drawn massive crowds especially in the F.A. Cup Match against Queens Park Rangers. Three star players excelled, Jimmy Boswell, Jackie Briggs and Hughie Russell.

The team 1947/48 with Top Row L. to R. Archie Clarke (Manager) and Eddie Fletcher (Secretary). Bottom Row L. to R. Albert Weller (Dir), Sid Martin (Dir) and Charles Cox (V.C.), Harry Woods (Dir) and Danny O'Donnell (Trainer).

1950.

April 1950.

Sporting Record, Week ending May 28, 1949

CLUB NOTICES

GILLINGHAM F.C., LTD. First-class Players required for all positions. Applications to Manager, Priestfield Stadium, Gillingham, Kent.

*

Gillingham, Southern League champions, after a hard fight with Chelmsford and Merthyr, are retaining all their first-team players.

Champions twice, and runners-up once in three years, Gillingham intend to strengthen their attack for next season. Past results have been obtained largely through a fine and consistent defence.

*

SUNDAY EMPIRE NEWS, November 30, 1947

Gillingham Refuse £30,000

FOLLOWING the refusal of £20,000 by Southend for Dudley, their centre-forward, and Montgomery, the half-back, Gillingham, the Kent League club, have just turned down an offer of £30,000 for six of their players.

The six are Russell, the young centre-forward several of the First League clubs are after, Warsap, Poole, Briggs, Forrester and Boswell.

The big amount offered for these men is as surprising as the refusal of it, for all except Russell are little more than just useful players.

Gillingham News

* * *

As part of their canvassing campaign in an attempt to regain League status Gillingham F.C. have circulated an attractive brochure, similiar to that issued last year to all present League members. Many of the club's supporters were able to purchase copies last year and they know what a wealth of information the brochure contained. The latest edition is just as informative as its predecessor and should prove an important propaganda weapon in the "Back to the League" campaign. Says Mr. Charles Cox (the club chairman) in asking the League clubs for their support: "We do not appeal to your sentiment as an old League Club, but rather to your good judgment and business acumen that Gillingham are a 'live' proposition." The brochure concludes: "Our policy upon re-election to the Third Division of the Football League would be to build up a team capable of reaching First Division strength. Our team has built up a reputation not only for its skill, but also for its sporting and clean football. Whether we are re-elected or not, we shall maintain that reputation."

WILL ADAMS.

TWO GILLINGHAM SUPPORTERS paraded outside the Cafe Royal, London, with sandwich boards as the delegates arrived for the annual meeting on Saturday.

Manager Archie Clark referring to Russell in an interview with a Sunday Newspaper said, "at the heading business he is nearly up to Dixie Dean standard and certainly as good as Tommy Lawton. I have played with them both."

It came as a bitter blow to the thousands of fans that Gillingham had to continue its spell in the wilderness of Southern League Football for at the Annual Meeting of the Football League in London their application for election to Third Division football did not even receive consideration.

With the start of the 1948 season one bears in mind Gerry Summers' remarks (see later). After you have had two wonderful seasons success becomes the norm and any slight failure seems a disaster. The team lost a few games and the cynics began to bleat, but the team fought on and were fourth in October. On the 14th of that month 'it took more than three hours of negotiation at Luton before Archie Clark was able to secure the signatures of three new players, the Burtonshaws and Collins, the latter being a "fine, natural footballer; equally strong in defence and attack." ' This was a record transfer bill for Gillingham and worked out at about £10,000 which necessitated an overdraft of £3,000. Even so the Club was in good spirits. The team was superb, the ground had been at last levelled, concrete terracing existed, turnstiles had been built and old debts paid. The present Director and then Vice Chairman Joe Leitch remembers vividly the era. "We were getting anything from 16,000 to 18,000 gates and I can remember the efforts which were being made behind closed doors in respect of our proposed application, once again, to join the League."

OBSERVER

FRIDAY, JUNE 9th, 1950

GLAD TO SEE YOU BACK "GILLS"—VERY

TOWNS BACK ON SOCCER MAP

But the "Gills" are faced with stern task

By DON ELLIS

NOW that the champagne corks have stopped popping and the excitement has begun to die down, it is as well to pause awhile and study the more practical aspects of Gillingham's return to League football.

The celebration that followed news of the "Gills" re-admission to the Third Division was amply justified.

CHAIRMAN W. S. C. COX

It was very definitely an occasion and one that called for rejoicing in a very big way.

Officials and supporters of the club were naturally jubilant. Business people, too, were not slow to realise the importance and possibilities of once more having a League club in the district.

But there is more to it than just that.

When I congratulated Mr. Charles Cox, the "Gills" chairman, immediately after the declaration of the ballot that had ended the Gillingham club's 12 years in the soccer wilderness, I asked him, "What does it feel like to be the chairman of a League club?"

"It feels fine," he replied, "but now our worries begin."

He was right. It is going to be a worrying time for all concerned with the management of the Priestfield Stadium club. The responsibilities of League football are much greater than those associated with the non-League brand of soccer.

FULLY AWARE

That the Gillingham directors were fully aware of their new responsibilities was evident, even at the informal celebration luncheon which they staged in London.

Underlying all the gaiety and the understandable verbal back slapping was a note, not so much of caution as of realisation that a tremendous added responsibility had that day been placed in their hands.

That this would be so had always been realised by Mr. Cox, his fellow directors and manager Archie Clark.

They had invited it and were prepared to accept it. So much so that they were not willing to blink the facts; even at a function that was largely an occasion for rejoicing.

Back home, the more enthusiastic among the "Gills" supporters were talking on the lines of emulating Charlton Athletic and reaching the First Division in three seasons!

In London, Mr. Cox, vice-chairman Joe Leech, and other speakers made no secret of the "Gills" ultimate aim—the provision of even better class football in the Medway Towns.

THEY ARE REALISTS

They did not, however, allow enthusiasm to run away with commonsense. They will put first things first.

And the first and most pressing need will be the provision of a team capable of taking its place in the Third Division when the new season opens on August 19th.

Manager Clark, I am sure, does not expect to set the Third Division alight in the "Gills" first season, or their second either, come to that.

For a couple of seasons, at least, it will be a question of settling down and building a team that will command a reasonably good league position. Somewhere about half-way in the table would be quite a fair start.

Naturally, the "Gills" are expecting very much bigger "gates" for Third Division football. Anything up to 20,000, I should say.

GROUND IMPROVEMENTS

The comfort of these spectators will be one of the chief considerations of the directors.

They will have to consider more covered accommodation, better and bigger stand facilities, more terracing on the slopes.

Other improvements will also become desirable as time goes on.

Naturally, all this cannot be accomplished all at one time.

Of necessity it will have to be treated as something of a long term policy. As will that First Division aim.

First and foremost, the "Gills" will go out to get the team. This will not be exactly an easy task. There is a general shortage of first class players, with transfer fees touching fantastic heights.

Fortunately the "Gills" have at least the nucleus of a reasonably sound side. They will naturally require quite a number of new players to fill certain gaps, and I feel sure that the directors will now insist on a largely full-time playing staff.

This will be essential to meet the sterner test of Third Division football.

Properly organised training, coaching and practice games are an essential to success in modern competitive football.

Already, Manager Clark is engaged on the search for new players. He knows the type of men required and will do his best to see the club gets them.

The "Gills" then, will go forward with high hopes. The task ahead will call for courage and determination.

Disappointments and setbacks there almost certainly will be from time to time, but given the right kind and volume of support there is no reason at all why the club should not firmly re-establish itself in the realm of League football.

It may take a little time, but the possibilities are there and should not be allowed to slip.

The Towns are back on the soccer map.

Let all co-operate to keep them there.

A CIVIC WELCOME BY THE MAYOR OF GILLINGHAM (Councillor G. M. Pinfold) to the Gillingham F.C. directors and officials when they reached the borough boundary, after they had succeeded in getting the "Gills" back into League football.

Again the team won the League title but were not elected to the Third Division. What did one have to do? They had lost only twenty games in three seasons, won the title twice, been runners-up once and scored some three hundred goals.

Being placed fifth in 1949/50 was no disgrace; surely with all the 'behind closed doors' work, good results and gates plus a greatly improved ground, the League Mandarins would now look favourably on the application. Publicity was good, and enthusiasm was mounting in the Medway Towns with the belief that at the next meeting of the Football League on the 27th March, 1950 they would agree with the proposal that two extra clubs should be taken into each of the Third Sections to cater for those teams worthy of league status. At that time outstanding claims in the South were Colchester and Gillingham.

At a meeting of high drama at the Café Royal, with sandwich board men picketing outside in favour of the 'Gills' it was finally agreed that there would be admission of four clubs to the League and thus each of the Third Divisions, North and South, was increased from twenty-two to twenty-four. Then there came the ballot as to which clubs should be included; Gillingham received forty-four votes, and Colchester twenty-eight, so both went into the League Football.

A civic welcome was effected by the Mayor for the Directors and Officials when they reached the Borough boundaries after succeeding in getting the 'Gills' back into the Football League after twelve long years. However Chairman Charles Cox was the first to admit "It feels fine but now our worries begin." The responsibility of League Football was much greater for the Club than that associated with the non-league brand of soccer.

The first thing which had to be undertaken was to provide a team capable of taking its place in the Third Division when the new season opened in August 1950. The Club would have to consider more covered accommodation, better and bigger stand facilities, more terracing on the slopes and other improvements. But still the enthusiasm was there. A sports writer of the time stated "the Towns are back on the soccer map. Let's all co-operate to keep them there."

Moving into the transfer market, Clark spent £10,000 purchasing Lewin, a full back, Gage, a goalkeeper and Ayers, an inside left. Shortly afterwards came Randolph Jenkins, a young inside forward with Fulham and then the Irish centre half Michael Skivington from Leyton Orient plus Robert Veck, an outside left from Southampton.

A pre-match cup of tea at Yeovil c.1950. Joe Leech top left corner/Eddie Fletcher (glasses) the Secretary, and Archie Clarke Manager (top right corner) with the players.

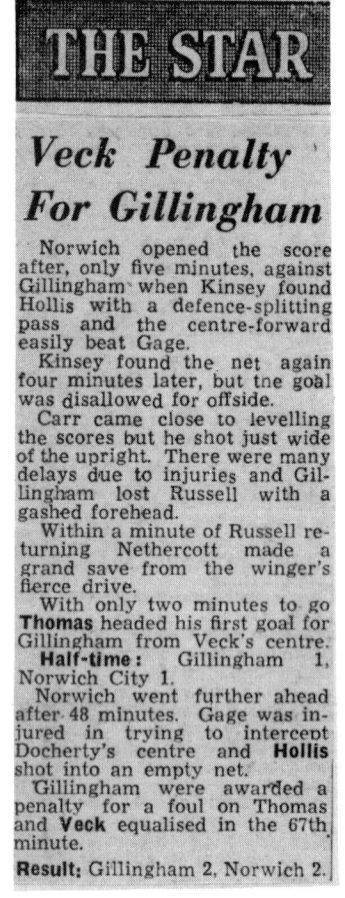

Veck Penalty For Gillingham

Norwich opened the score after, only five minutes, against Gillingham when Kinsey found Hollis with a defence-splitting pass and the centre-forward easily beat Gage.

Kinsey found the net again four minutes later, but the goal was disallowed for offside.

Carr came close to levelling the scores but he shot just wide of the upright. There were many delays due to injuries and Gillingham lost Russell with a gashed forehead.

Within a minute of Russell returning Nethercott made a grand save from the winger's fierce drive.

With only two minutes to go **Thomas** headed his first goal for Gillingham from Veck's centre.

Half-time: Gillingham 1, Norwich City 1.

Norwich went further ahead after 48 minutes. Gage was injured in trying to intercept Docherty's centre and **Hollis** shot into an empty net.

Gillingham were awarded a penalty for a foul on Thomas and **Veck** equalised in the 67th minute.

Result: Gillingham 2, Norwich 2.

Training 50's style — short hair and long shorts. A young Bill Collins can be seen fourth from right, in the front rank.

There was an air of excitement as the beginning of the season drew near; to help their four new Clubs the Football League waived one of its wage payment rules that no first season league pofessional could earn more than £7 per week. Accordingly Gillingham decided to pay their top professionals the maximum of £12 per week — exactly what Stanley Matthews was getting at the time!

The season started well and a crowd of 20,000 paid nearly £1,500 to see a draw with Colchester in torrential rain; the first league victory was quite brilliant and came on the 2nd September with four goals in sixteen minutes against Millwall before another 20,000 enthusiastic spectators. Bill Collins remembers the game well. "It was probably the most enjoyable game I ever had with Gillingham. Probably one of the most exciting. What was particularly ironic was that at half time, Archie Clark told us to go in and defend even though we were four goals up! He had a few words with us and said that as far as he was concerned the score was still 0-0. In the second half we did defend and they put three goals past us!"

But things did not go as well as expected even with the signing of Dave Thomas from Watford and accordingly Manager Clark decided in November 1950 to adopt new training tactics; sprinting was to form the basis of the Gills' future with far less ball work. This did not pay off and on the 22nd November they crashed 9-2 to Nottingham Forest. Surviving a 'Dunkirk' after travelling to Bristol Rovers for the cup they nearly snatched a win in the replay at Priestfield. The team then went to White Hart Lane and in a blinding snow storm Bristol won by the odd goal. The teams were 1-1 with four minutes remaining to play when Petherbridge, Rovers' outside right, flicked the ball first time toward the Gillingham goal, Lewin the Gills' left back was standing just inside the penalty area and it struck his arm. Three hundred minutes of hard slogging by both sides was ended by the penalty kick.

A swamping of Exeter City in January 1951 did not help the situation and the season 50/51 finished with Plymouth Argyle beating the Gills 2-1 and the team finishing third from bottom having played forty-six matches and having conceded a hundred and one goals.

During the close season there was talk of fresh purchases and Manager Clark said, "We are not rushing in to pay the big prices that are being asked at the moment. Things may get a little easier later on and then we may be able to make a move." Clark desperately wanted a centre half and

August 1953. Morgan, Marks, Boswell, Rigg, Lewin, Durkin, Scarth, Forrester, Niblett, Evans, Long.

1958/59 Top Row L. to R. Parry, Hughes, Simpson, Edgar, Proverbs, Laing; Bottom Row Pulley, Tudor, Bacon, Hannaway, Patrick.

continued "If I can fill that satisfactorily I honestly believe we can have a much better season." And in fact it did not start off badly at all. The first game was a 1-1 draw with Millwall which was creditable but not exceptional; there was some other good games, beating Torquay 3-0 and Portvale 4-2 and about October 1951 the Gills were seventh in the League. Four goals against Swindon Town in that month excited 15,700 which included at least three local Parliamentary candidates. At this time Derek Lewis was the leading scorer in the Third Division South with fourteen goals to his credit and some say that at the time he was perhaps the most brilliant young outside right in the Country. In November Dave Thomas got his hundredth league goal in a draw with Watford. These were only pin pricks of light, however, in what turned out to be a rather disappointing season.

Perhaps the next year was of most consequence as a result of Jimmy Scarth's registering one of the best goal scoring efforts in football history. He scored a hat trick in two and a half minutes in November 1952 against Leyton Orient but again the team escaped relegation by the skin of their teeth. It was all or nothing in the last game of the season against Bristol City. With so much at stake Gillingham attacked from the kick-off before a 12,000 gate which showed striking evidence of loyalty by the fans. The game had to be won and Gillingham went out to win it. Inspired by skipper Vic Niblett in defence and veteran Dave Thomas in attack the Gills played a brand of football that was almost a revelation.

Thomas made the first goal, going to the left to take up a pass from Ayers; the Gillingham centre forward sailed past two defenders with "almost nonchalant ease" before putting a low ball across to Billy Burtonshaw who was able to side foot it into the net. Next Forrester made the score 2-0 after Scarth had seen his volley rebound off a Bristol defender. After half time Thomas chested down a ball and hammered it in and shortly afterwards came the goal of the match. Scarth centered and Thomas, with his back to the goal, turned deftly to score the fourth. The fifth and final goal came in the seventy-fourth minute; a Briggs centre confused the City defence and enabled Burtonshaw to drive the ball home. Roars of delight greeted the final whistle and the fans left the ground to the appropriate tune 'I'll see you again'.

Clark decided to rebuild his team and purchased Tony Blake and Frank McKee from Birmingham City, then Ken Lambert from Barnsley. Two more signings followed, Paddy Sowden and Harold Korman, both from Hull. Then came Maurice Morecroft, a twenty-two-year-old goalkeeper from Sheffield United and Trevor Long from Wolves. Bad news arrived in the middle of July when it was found that the extremely popular Hugh Russell, after five years with the Club, would have to leave professional football following an injury which he had received at Easter 1952. Having been advised by a specialist that he could no longer go on with the game he formally retired. He had been seen by Archie Clark playing for the Royal Engineers with friends Vic Hole, Jackie Briggs, George Forrester and Jimmy Boswell, all of whom had come to Gillingham. Perhaps one of the most popular players ever to grace the Gillingham pitch, he was sorely missed.

Clark's purchases which included George King from Bradford City and Trevor Lewis from Coventry had little or no effect and the team continued to wallow in the lower regions of the division.

During February 1953 discussions ensued as to whether the club should have floodlights. Vice Chairman Joe Leech said, "I don't think there is any future in it at all, unless there is a congested fixture list. . . for the public to stand out on the terraces at night in cold or wet weather may be more than we can expect. As a spectacle I don't doubt for one moment it would be an attraction for a little while but the novelty would wear off." Mr Leech now laughs at this statement "I was wrong" he says. He was however in good company for Archie Clark is quoted as saying, "I don't think floodlighting would ever come to competitive football. Football is the working man's Saturday afternoon entertainment. There will be plenty of opposition to floodlit football from the theatres, cinemas, dog racing and speedway racing."

The '50s show a Manager of some power and personality coping with dismal results interspersed with exceptional skill. The Board having entered the Football League after good results in the Southern League, were faced with a trebled wage bill and figures show that gates generally began to fall off in the mid '50s.

The '40s had been an exciting time, the '50s were not going well. In their eight seasons in the Third Division in only one did they score more goals than their opponents and that was when they came fourth in 1954/55. The team had entertained and produced exciting and effective football in many games. They had, however, lacked the ability to live with the others over the whole league programme.

In June 1958, Archie Clark left after nearly twenty years of being with the Club, just as the team entered the recently created League Division Four. Harry Barratt replaced him to take on the job of preparing the team for the '60s.

A selection of cartoons by G.R. Prince, 1951.

Chapter 6

The sixties started in what may be termed an average way, but by the fourth season Harry Barratt's men had settled into 20th position and he left in early 1962 being replaced by Freddie Cox, the former Manager of Portsmouth and ex-Arsenal and Spurs winger.

Taking over in the middle of a bribes probe and during another financial crisis, in his first week at Priestfield Stadium he set up a new regime which involved substantial stamina training including road runs and gymnasium workouts. At the start of the season Cox's enthusiasm had proved contagious which resulted in an increased demand for season tickets.

After winning their first game 2-1, against Chester, the team lost 4-1 to Brentford and the Press commented "Gillingham have done it again! It is an old, old custom at Priestfield Stadium to bolster the hopes of supporters and then let them down with a bump that shakes the whole area."

It is worth, just for a moment, to take a breather here. After mediocrity (sometimes caressing disaster) for so many years, a fresh face comes along. Both fans and Press expect him not only to perform miracles but to do them especially on Saturday afternoons. After all the fanfare, the team has played a few games and the Press jump on the Manager because the results are not as good as expected. Surely even the most mentally inadequate must realise that it takes years, not weeks, to build a team, give it faith in itself, teach it to work as a unit and train players to interact with each other. No wonder Gerry Summers calls it "a ridiculous profession."

However, Gillingham moved to third place in the fourth division in September 1962 and at the same time received a letter from the Football League notifying them that their enquiries regarding alleged bribes had proved negative. The Club was "pleased to hear that the matter is now concluded." With the smear cleared up a weight was lifted from the Board of Directors.

By November 1962 the team were sixth, having defeated Oldham 4-3 in a match which Director Charles Cox described as "Wonderful, Wonderful!!" The good spell continued with a 4-0 defeat of Crewe. By the beginning of 1963, the National Press rated three Gillingham players as outstanding. Campbell as left back, Pulley as outside left and Farrall as left half. Notwithstanding such success, gates were well down on previous years and even when the team moves up to fifth in the Table they could only get 5,000 supporters. This is not to say that Gillingham were having any more problems than other clubs during the early sixties. An extract from 'The Times' throws some light on the problems. "The hard core of genuine support remains, yet even this section is now having its undivided loyalty taxed by counter attractions. . . in a world of changing social habit, increased activities, wider distribution of prosperity, the week-end family car, etc. – the man on the terrace has become more selective. Mediocrity is harder to sell now." The supporter was becoming more of a customer and less of a fan.

About this time to cope with the changing pattern of the game one sees a movement towards the spectacularisation which probably was one of the reasons for the acquisition of the floodlights in August 1963. The first game played under these lights against Bury drew the biggest crowd for years, then 17,500 crammed into the new floodlit Priestfield Stadium for a top of the Table clash with Carlisle United. Not only the ground itself was crowded, the streets for quite a long way in all directions were tightly packed. Things were definitely looking up. The Gills scored their first goal in just forty-five seconds (Ron Newman) and the second from George Francis in the second half clinched it. The team on that day were Simpson, Hudson, Hunt, Arnott, Burgess, Farrall, Newman, Stringfellow, Francis, Gibbs and Pulley. The season 1963/4 was proving excellent and even though Gillingham were knocked out of the League Cup by

The team 1962-63
Smith, Vaessen, Livesey, McIntyre, Simpson, Huddart
Hughes, Challis, Farrall, O'Donnell (Trainer)
Waldock, Wright, F. Cox, Hunt, Ridley, Pulley
Amato, Godfrey, Matthews

Leicester who had playing with them a young Frank McClintock, the week afterwards they steamed back and put three goals past Workington in a vital match. There was furtive talk of champagne in the Boardroom at the end of the season.

Valuable points were gained steadily during January 1964 but now the pressure and tension was building up and a 1-1 draw with Doncaster at Priestfield caused hearts to quiver and a plethora of letters decrying the Gills' efforts. The fans were now expecting the best and second best was just not good enough. A barrage of criticism hit the club after they drew six of seven matches and Freddie Cox, who had previously made comments such as "You would think we were bottom of the Division" became ruthless and dropped many regulars from the side — which in fact led to a 2-0 defeat at Brighton! Again the team played exceedingly well in what turned out to be a seething cauldron of excitement as more than 15,000 fans screamed their support for the two teams striving mightily for the winning goal.

In great urgency Cox signed John Meredith from Chesterfield just in time to do nothing, for football came to a standstill due to a particularly severe winter. Even during this breather the tension was at breaking point as one can see from what would now seem a virtual totalitarian statement made by Manager Cox to the Daily Mirror. "I want to make it perfectly clear that players should not expect to get married in the football season. If you are in the hunt for promotion or fighting against relegation, you can't afford to have any diversions." He was so firm on this point that he planned to get a clause to that effect written into the players' contract for future seasons. Shades of the past here surely!

Nerves and stuttering form didn't help the championship prospects; a 3-1 win over Barrow was followed by a loss against Workington (1-0) but then a 2-0 win over Oxford pushed the Gills into second place with two games in hand. Exeter City was still leading with 55 points and the Gills second, on goal average with 54. Theoretically the club needed seven points from their last five games to ensure promotion to the Third Division although the Manager thought that four would do the trick.

It all came down to the final game between Rochdale and York and the players had to wait for the result which was a Saturday evening match. A few hours after the match, champagne corks did in fact pop when the club found itself going into the Third Division as a result of York City's 1-0 win. Now they were certain of promotion the aim was the championship and a thirty-first minute goal by centre forward Francis beat Newport 1-0, so snatching the title on goal average over Carlisle United. During that season the Gills played forty-six games, won twenty-three, drew fourteen, and lost nine. They had scored 59 goals and conceded 30. Second in the Table Carlisle had scored 113 goals (oh for those days of old!) but had conceded more.

When a team wins promotion the first thought of fans is 'can we do it again next year?' Now in the Third Division the feeling was that Second Division football would shortly be on its way and the crowds increased with this thought in mind.

It was not to be, even though the team played with distinction between 1964 and 1968 finishing seventh, sixth, eleventh and twelfth respectively. As the team worked on the field so the Directors worked off it and ideas were formulated for an £80,000 'Priestfield Plan', a new stand, costing £54,000, a floodlit allweather surface for training to be used as a car park on match days, a boundary wall and so on. Nor did they neglect the players' future, agreeing to support Good, Moss and Taylors' application to the Football League for a grant of £60 to undertake a course in Ladies' Hairdressing.

Freddie Cox after guiding the club out of the doldrums and in to respectability left in January 1966 to take over the Managership of Bournemouth and Basil Hayward, then with Bedford Town, took over after a number of discussions with Dr Grossmark, who had become Chairman.

Outside influences were now beginning to tell on football generally. There were pressures which both Manager, Players and Directors had not experienced in the past. The supporter had become a television addict and as such demanded good entertainment on Saturday afternoons. He could travel more freely and would go to London to see a game if it was to be one of high quality. The idea of spectacularisation had not necessarily taken place at the level of the game

POST OFFICE TELEGRAM

GILLINGHAM FOOTBALL CLUB CENTRAL HOTEL
GILLINGHAMKENT=

CONGRATULATIONS LADS = THREE FEMALE SUPPORTERS

CHT71 12.35 CHATHAM T 11 BV CPY

BEST WISHES TO YOUR TEAM FOR SUCCESS IN TONIGHTS MATCH FOR DIVISION FOUR CHAMPIONSHIP= KENT POLICE +

WELL DONE CONGRATULATIONS = GPO SUPPORTERS

12.0 ROCHESTERKENT 12 R R BV

THANKS FOR JUSTIFYING MY CONFIDENCE GREAT SHOW =
OLD-UN ++

The Chairman receives the trophy from Joe Richards, President of the Football League at the Café Royal, June 1964.

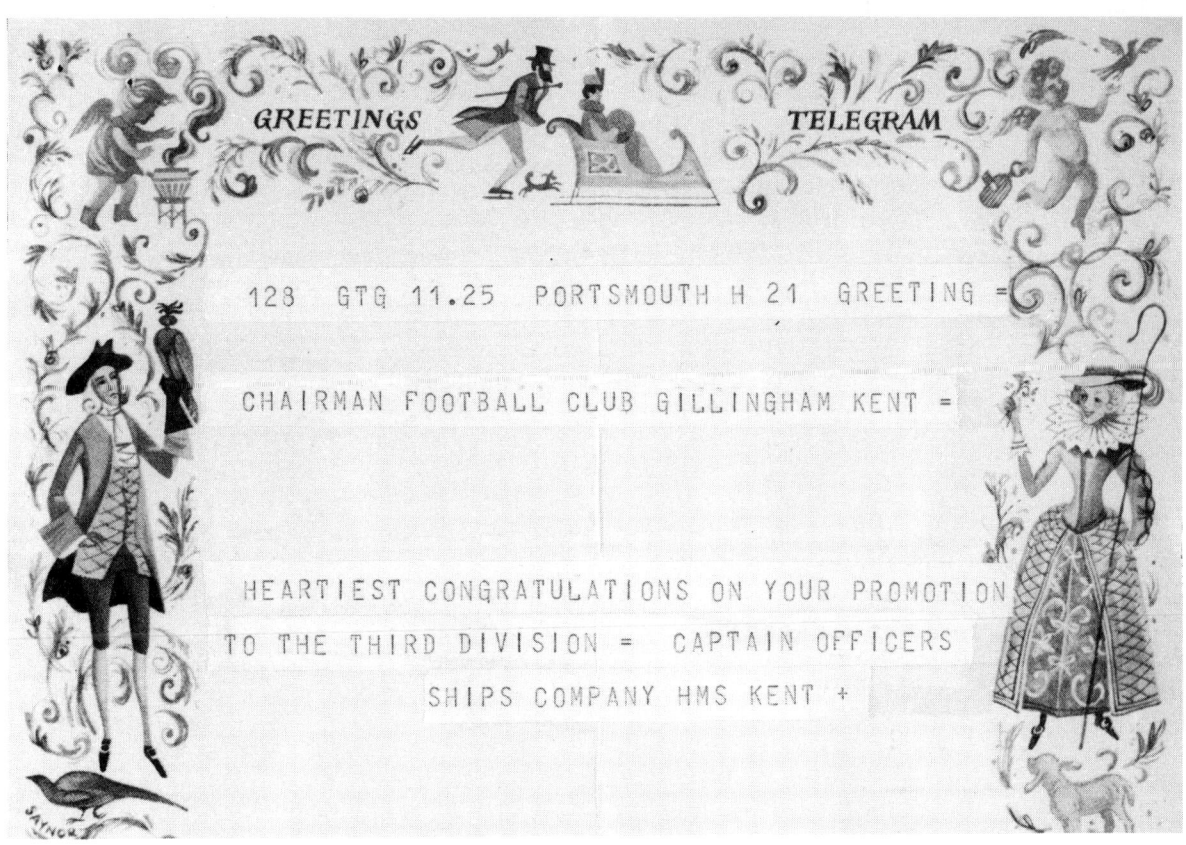

The team 1968/69
Simpson, Riddick, Williams, Bailey, Gilbert, Simmons, Boswell
Gibbs, Thear, Green, Simpson, Belotti, Quirke, Hall, Folds, Hayward (Manager)
Woodley, Machin, Yeo, Meredith, Osborn, Weston
Robbins, Tydeman, Bray, Peach

itself but in the relationship between the game and the media. The television had changed the football match into a spectacle 'designed for passive consumption'.

In addition the classic footballer was no longer the Stanley Matthews type. Examination of perhaps the greatest footballer in English history shows 'he was the opposite of glamorous. A non-drinker, non-smoker, careful with his money, brought up among thrift and the ever looming threat of dole and debt. . .!' The new footballer was emerging in the late sixties; no longer was the high point of his life retirement from the game and the hope of becoming a local publican or sports shop owner.

From the mid sixties to the early seventies is one of Dr. Grossmarks' grey if not black periods. So poor were the team's results in the late sixties and in 1970 that a special meeting of the supporters' association was held when both Basil Hayward and Dr. Grossmark were present to answer supporters' questions. In due course Basil Hayward resigned owing to severe criticism.

Relegation from the Third Division in the season 1970/71 after the euphoria of the 63/64 season was a tragic but foreseeable disaster. Between 1967 and 1971 the team had again achieved the distinction of having more goals being conceded each season than those scored, and having won only 53 games from a possible 138. It fell to Andy Nelson to attempt rectification.

Chapter 7

If one were to prepare a graph, based on Gillingham's record since inception, it would resemble the Alps, heights of success interposed with troughs of failure. Yet the philosphically inclined will remark that 'Surely the Alps are better to look at than say, the flat landscape of Holland?'

From their first season in Division Four the team faced another Alp, but they were to prove worthy mountaineers. The new Manager, Andy Nelson, had no real experience in the Managerial field but to all intents was a good coach and had been involved with Sir Alf Ramsey during his successful days at Ipswich. The style adopted, on paper at least, was very much the 'softly, softly, catchee monkee' and his approach was initially to try and build an atmosphere of confidence. His first season was not terribly promising, the Club finished thirteenth, although the gates had increased by an average of 1,000 for each game. 1972/73 showed a real improvement and for the first time since 1966 Gillingham scored more goals than they conceded; it was only five more (63-58) but at least it was a move in the right direction and at the end of the season they finished a respectable ninth, with the vaguest murmurings of 'next year you see. . . ' being heard whenever supporters gathered.

And so a new season dawned and immediately things began to gel. As Londoners would say the team was 'looking tasty'. Dick Tydeman got his hundred-and-fiftieth goal in a superb victory over Swansea and then followed a real piece of exhibition football in the total destruction of Scunthorpe by seven goals to two which put the Club seventh in the Table and within striking distance of the title. By mid November with a 4-0 win over Workington moving them into third position the murmurings had become shouts. It look right. It felt right. We were on our way!

Andy Nelson, like all Managers, played it cautious "I'm delighted. . . but there's still a lot to do." The supporters thought otherwise and the gates leaped from an average of 3,000 in the season 1972/73 to 7,000. By the New Year, with just seven matches to go, according to accounts the fans were treated to a spectacular game against Peterborough ". . . which made a mockery of third division football, both sides attacked each other fiercely from the kick-off. After fifty seven minutes Dave Coxhill, although suffering from a back injury, collected the ball on the edge of the area, spotted a gap and slipped it through. Richardson, who had been having a wonderful game up front had only 'keeper Steel to beat but full-back Lee opted to make the scoring more difficult by hauling the Irishman to the ground. The subsequent penalty was scored by Lindsey." And the Press were not slow to point out that on that day 12,000 people turned up to watch the Gills, some 2,000 more than watched the England International team playing Portugal in Lisbon.

With their power up front, effective defence and terrific team spirit by now the Medway was believing that Third Division Football would return. But though there had been a change in the team's attitude from the previous season, the fans were not pleased at all by the suggestion that there should be a change in the teams colours, and Andy Nelson, under public pressure, dropped the idea of playing in red and blue.

Scoring goals prolifically, ninety in all, Gillingham finished second in the Table and were accordingly promoted to the Third Division. What makes a team tick? What motivates them? Such are the unanswered questions in a season such as 1973/74. The year before they had been little more than a below average side but within months had occurred a metamorphosis and they were now virtually supermen. Alan Hodgkinson considers success sustains itself; Gerry Summers takes the view that one or two signings can make all the difference. The team had

DIRECTORS MEETING HELD AT THE REGISTERED OFFICES, PRIESTFIELD STADIUM, GILLINGHAM, TUESDAY 4th NOVEMBER, 1975.

PRESENT:- Dr. C.S. GROSSMARK, in the Chair.
Messrs C.A.L. Cox, B.B. Moore and A.E. Weller.
Manager, Mr G. Summers and Club Secretary, M. Bramley.

RESIGNATION OF MANAGER & TRAINER

The Chairman reported that the Manager Mr L. Ashurst and Trainer Mr L. Toms had resigned from the Club on Wednesday 15th October to take up an appointment with Sheffield Wednesday Football Club. It was confirmed that the Club Solicitor has written to Sheffield Wednesday regarding the matter of financial compensation for the remaining period of Mr Ashurst's contract.

APPOINTMENT OF MANAGER.

The Chairman reported that Mr G. Summers had accepted the position of Manager with effect from the 28th October at a salary of _____ per annum. It was confirmed that Mr Summers had agreed to sign a three year contract.
The Chairman and Directors welcomed the Manager to the meeting and expressed their wish that Mr Summers should have a long and successful

Listening to the manager: Henderson, Price, Ford, Overton and Wetherley. Opposite: The page from the minute book recording the appointment of Gerry Summers.

been most spectacular, and the last time they obtained more than 62 points had been in the season 1948/49. A civic reception heralded a new era.

But then came a nasty shock. The extremely popular Andy Nelson left for Charlton to be replaced by Len Ashurst. He received a mixed reception due to the immense popularity of Nelson and his effect on the Club was to be ephemeral as he left within a short period, moving to Sheffield Wednesday.

Ashurst's leaving came as a great surprise to all in the area; he had built a side which at his time of leaving occupied fifth place in Division Three and although it was allegedly boring and stereotyped it did prove effective. For a short while Bill Collins took over and then the Club acquired the services of Gerry Summers who had been the Manager of Oxford United. Said Dr. Grossmark the Chairman after Mr. Summers had joined the Club, "It has been the worst time of my life. Gerry Summers had been our original choice. He did not apply for the job but was tracked down and signed up. He was first on the list."

Officially meeting the staff on the 28th October 1975, Mr. Summers led his team, ironically, against Sheffield Wednesday managed by Len Ashurst on the 5th November and the Gills lost 1-0. From all accounts they played superbly and to add to the irony Neil O'Donnell, the former Gills player who had up to the sixty-ninth minute contributed little to the game sent a pass between central defenders Dave Shipley and Dave Wiltshire for Joicy to run through and score.

The new Manager worked hard with the team and in the season 1977/78 they finished a more than respectable seventh in the League with 50 points.

Although no one knew it at the time the season 1978/79 was to be one of the most exciting in the Club's history. They got close enough to smell the turf of Second Division Clubs. At the end of the season promotion to the Second Division evaded the team and the disappointment was felt not only by the players, officials and supporters but by virtually the whole of the Medway Towns. However the season was not a failure, the Gills' final position was their highest ever and even those who had never been within a mile of the Stadium suddenly became experts. A bumper crowd of 15,000 turned up for the game against promotion rivals Shewsbury — the Third Division's eventual champions — who lost 2-0. This was the Club's biggest home gate for thirteen years and hundreds swarmed onto the pitch at the end of the game to cheer Manager Gerry Summers and his team. That game was probably the high point of the season; the team eventually obtained 59 points and I have no doubt that if anyone had told the Manager, in the January, that that was how many they were to get he would have assumed promotion. The Gills came fourth. Teams had been promoted in the past with 57 or even 56 points. Beaten only eight times, one more point and it would have meant the Second Division. They should have won irritating games such as that at Colchester after being two up; and then there were the two home games against Rotherham and Carlisle which were at the most one-sided draws. But it was a "mad time" with new men brought into the side after injuries to key players (Graham Knight and Charlie Young were both missing for virtually the whole season with Damien Richardson and John

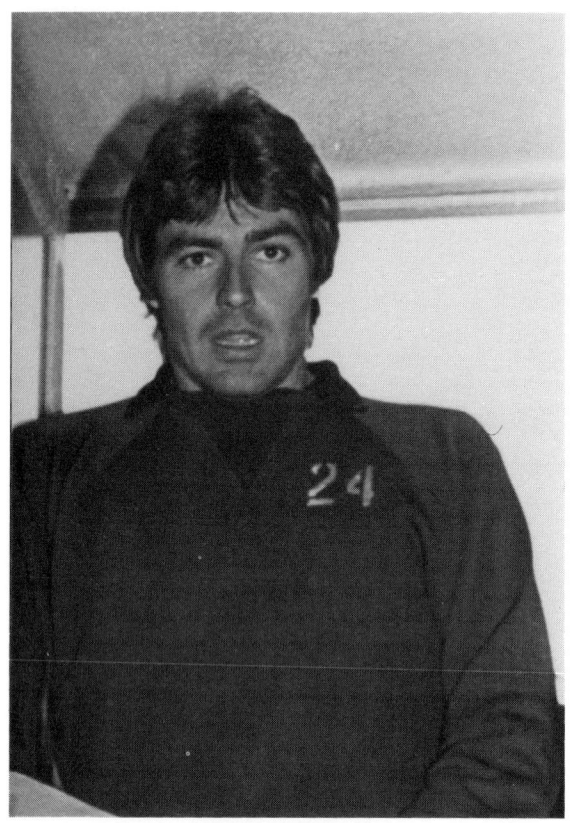
Mickey Barker.

Terry Jolly.

Billy Hughes.

Ken Price.

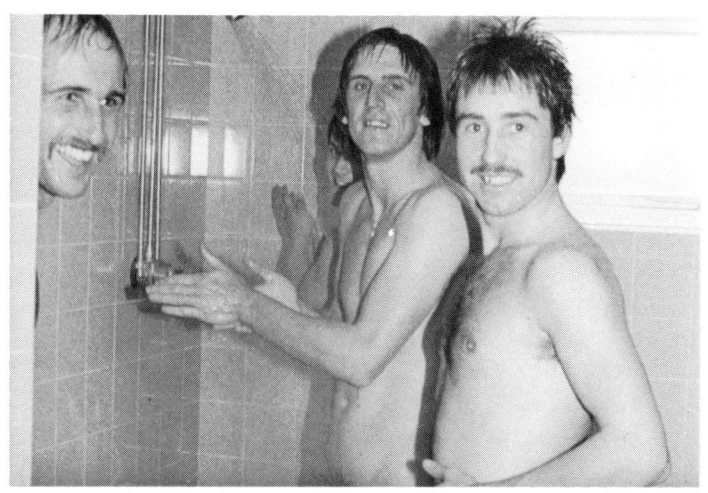

The New Boys, Ford, Henderson and Lloyd

Crabbe side-lined for the later stages). Mark Weatherley made an incredible impact when moved to central defence. John Sharpe and the exceptionally skilful new signing Micky Barker helped produce a defence which conceded fewer goals than any side except the champions Shrewsbury; Tony Funnell, a signing from Southampton, made an immediate hit with the supporters. It had been a truly wonderful season and the players had relished the atmosphere.

Gerry Summers knew that the next season would be difficult, "last season we had crept up quietly, now they will be expecting and gunning for us." And how do you keep up the impetus after so narrowly missing?

The new season opened and the Gills looked rather sharp in their warm up games. In a display against the then First Division leaders Norwich in the League Cup they were quite brilliant, outfighting, out-thinking, outplaying and outmanoeuvring their illustrious opponents at every stage. A goal came when Steve Bruce got up at the far post from a corner by Richardson and headed the kick backwards to Overton who headed beyond the helpless goalkeeper. Later a weak shot was deflected and landed on Taylor's foot. He moved forward a yard or two and lofted it over Hillyard's head which gave Norwich the equaliser. Sadly the team lost 4-2 at Norwich which ended their hopes in the League Cup, and after that erraticism (if there is such a word) set in. In October after a sorry 2-0 defeat at Mansfield the Gills destroyed Southend with three goals from Westwood, Bruce and Crabbe. A couple of draws were followed by a horror story at Sheffield United in November where four goals were conceded. On the 20th of that month at the Annual General Meeting the Manager explained that he had failed to sign anyone this season for two main reasons, firstly that the type of player he was seeking —experienced mid-field men — came few and far between and that fees had rocketed tenfold; secondly such players demanded very high wages. Dr. Grossmark informed the Meeting that the Club had made a working loss over the season ending 6th May but that was explained more easily when it was considered that the Club had paid out more than a £100,000 on three new players and some £50,000 on the new sports complex. There was, however, an overall net profit of £31,000 which was, in Dr. Grossmark's words, "A magnificent achievement." It was thus not necessary for Dr. Grossmark to allow sheep to graze on the pitch to pay some of the bills! By January/February results on the pitch had placed the Club in a precarious League position. March arrived and the Gills were faced with an away game on the 1st against top of the Table Grimsby. They lost 1-0 and faint hearts flickered; things were not going too well. In this day and age supporters expect miracles not from God but from Managers. There was now little hope of the Club joining the Second Division and when April arrived it drew showers both real and mental and there came a real threat of relegation — four losses on the trot created a danger of collapse, and the side just could not get into its stride. How strange those months were, for in December there had been talk of promotion and by May it was of relegation. So go the ups and downs of football.

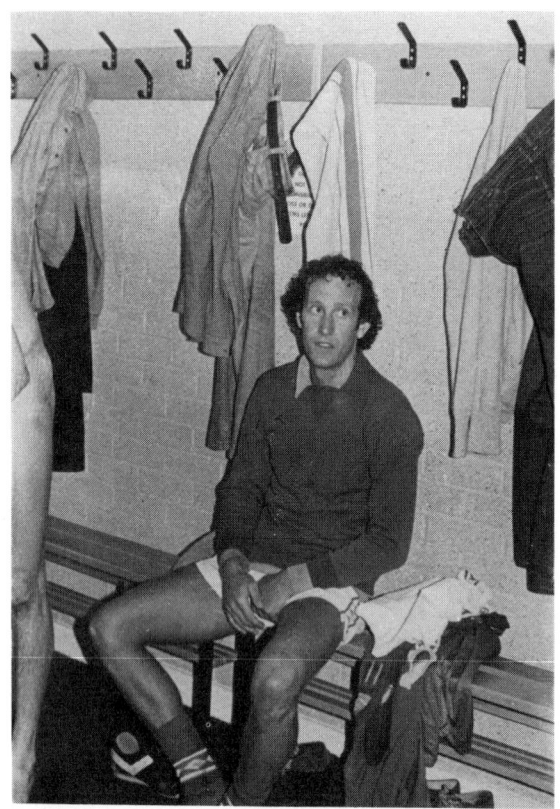
Ron Hillyard.

Nigel Donn.

Tony Bottiglieri.

John Sharpe.

Tony Funnell.

Garry Armstrong.

A minor crisis occurred with some eight players being put on the transfer list. And a ninth, Tony Funnell, the recent signing from Southampton being sold to Brentford for £55,000.

April 19th was a black day for Gillingham. There was a mountain of bad feelings existing between the supporters of Swindon and Gillingham but nearly a year had passed since the notorious events at the Swindon ground when fisticuffs had been the order of the day. Perhaps it went back even further to the famous Test Match in 1894 when as a result of beating Swindon Gillingham obtained promotion. Who knows. The game proved disastrous with Swindon scoring three goals and Steve Bruce being sent off.

The gates slumped and Priestfield could only record 3,479 people turning up to watch Rotherham beat them 1-0; the next game against Chester on the 30th April, was away. Despite a run of six matches without a win at last the Gills hit form with Crabbe and White scoring and the team producing a spirited performance with enough skill and talent to prove conclusively that they belonged to the Third Division.

It was, however, a sad end of the season when Plymouth beat Gillingham 1-0 in the last game at Priestfield before a crowd of a mere 4,000. Finishing sixteenth in the Table the team for that final game was Hillyard, Sharp, Overton, Bruce, Weatherley, Crabbe, White, Duncan, Richardson, Jolley and Adams, the substitute being Walker. So ended the season 1979/80.

In the close season, moving in to the transfer market, Gerry Summers acquired Lloyd, Henderson and Ford but it is too early to tell their full potential.

The new season begins and the question must be will they do it this year? No, that is not the way it should be said. Will WE do it this year? Will the Superblues roar into the Second Division or not? All is forgotten of last season as a fresh generation enters the ground. Whether we just missed going up or missed by a mile a new season is now a new chance. Unlike the average human being, a fresh start is given to a football team each year. Perhaps that is the key to its popularity?

Gerry Summers in action.

Extracts from Interviews
GERRY SUMMERS, MANAGER

Q. Tell me something about your background in football. Have you been in it all your life?
A. When I left school I had a job in insurance for a very short time, so really I have been in football all my life. I am a Midlander, born in Birmingham, and it was natural for me to play for one of the local clubs. I joined West Bromwich Albion; they had thirteen teams when I started and you had to work your way through these. I was with Don Howe at the time and we both went through the whole thirteen.
Q. What salary were you on when you started?
A. In those days we would have paid them to play!
Q. What were your best times in football and how did you get involved in coaching?
A. My best years were with Sheffield United during the time when we got as far as the semi-final of the F.A. Cup when we played Leicester (three times if I remember). That was the year they beat us and went on and lost to Spurs.

I took up coaching pretty early actually. I was just about to leave West Brom. for Sheffield United when I went on my first course with Ron Greenwood at Lillershall. I would have been about 21 or 22. I then went on for a few years and got my full badge. I was lucky enough, during the changeover from Walter Winterbottom to Alan Wade, who is now the F.A. Director of Coaching, to get recognised, and get involved with staff work. It was very good for me. I would play football all the year and during the summer would go to Lillershall during the courses.
Q. What do you think are the qualities necessary to be a good Manager?
A. Resiliance I think is one of the main things; and you've got to be a bit of a football fanatic, a keen student of the game (which I always was as a player, coach and Manager) and tremendously enthusiastic. You must be an enthusiast because this is such a ridiculous profession anyhow.
Q. Why is it ridiculous?
A. Well, because everything is stacked against you. For a start only a few of the ninety-two clubs can be successful and what might be success in one way is keeping a side in the league. But you get no recognition for that.

A manager also needs a sense of humour and a bad memory so he can forget the bad things. Also I suppose you have got to be a realist. You have got to accept that you are in a job which has a high casualty rate and you learn through experience the people you want to work for. In addition you have got to be realistic with yourself though, and there has got to be some give and take.

Plus, of course, and this is often forgotten, you have to have some administrative flair. The only people who have a couple of months off at the end of the season are players. The Manager's job is also administration, which carries on for the whole year. I have got to organise pre-season games, deal with players' contracts, organise the hotels for the away games, deal with the final recruitment of apprentices and players, talk to parents about boys and so on. At the moment, for example, we have Exeter early on in the season; as this is a holiday area we have to try and book the hotel as quickly as possible. I work closely with Richard Dennison in this respect and he takes quite a deal of administrative work off my hands. We have a very good working relationship which is vital.
Q. What do you find a difficult aspect of Managing?
A. One of the hardest things is the continual motivation of a team throughout the whole season. It's not like an athlete who prepares himself for just one race. Sometimes Managing and coaching is bloody sheer hard work when things are just not going right. On other occasions a team needs very little motivation at all. But you just can't shout and abuse people if the thing isn't going right. One of my strengths, I feel, is my consistency in what I put over to them. I believe in consistency and stability. They know that I am a footballing man and I am going to keep pleading and preaching football because long term I know that's the best way to do it.
Q. I hope I am making myself clear when I ask you what do you believe in? What would you, for example, call the Summers' ideology?
A. I am a footballing man. A lot of people accuse me sometimes of wanting to play too much football, but I believe that the game is all about what is happening at the top level. The Liverpools and Notts Forests have a lot of ball possession. It's about passing movement. I believe very much in these things. I want to pass the ball from one end to the other rather than whack it. I firmly believe in that and always have done. And I believe in the fitness of the players. Naturally I believe in skill but you have got to marry it with the physical capabilities of

a player. If you are looking at a football pitch it is a big area. Now how can you influence a game, if you are a player, on that big area without physical fitness? Work rate is an 'out' word in England at the moment. We all want to play skilfully. Now that's important, skill is important, but how is a fellow going to affect a game without putting himself about? We have a good side and they can put themselves about. They are mobile and hard working. One of our strengths is our mobility — being able to get from one end to the other very rapidly and quickly.

Q. What do you look for in a player? What are the qualities you think are necessary to succeed as a player?

A. There are a lot of things that make up a player but one of the biggest is attitude. Is he a hard worker? Is he aggressive enough? Naturally enough to go along with these things he has got to have a reasonable amount of skill. Although I don't wish to give any examples in the team it's particularly easy for me to mention Steve Bruce. He was turned down by clubs as a school boy, four in all, then we took him. He has had to fight all the way through his school football and after a lot of hard work from him and us he begins now to blossom out. So many of the youngsters fade away, whereas the Steve Bruces of this world have had competition all the way through since they were twelve or thirteen.

But I don't want to push the aggression thing too far. You want aggressive players because you know its about winning the ball, but you have got to mix aggression with skill; put the other side off their stride. When they are sticking their foot in you have got to stick your foot in. There is a fair bit of intimidation in professional football. I have experience of this having played against the Italians and by God what an experience that was. You know when you go over there you play — if you can! We had one International with us and I remember so well at the first corner he got up and headed the ball which hit the bar. He never got off the floor again, they just wouldn't let him.

Now get this right I don't go and say 'the first thing that you will do is to whack him!' However you are living in a situation where you know unless you are aggressive and can put the other side off their stride you won't be successful. The most important thing is for you to play but also to stop them playing. You have to have a bit of both. In the same way as there is a fine edge between success and failure, there is a fine edge between aggression and too much aggression. Aggression can be shown in running at opponents, forwards taking on defenders, and defenders wanting to break forward.

Q. What do you do at half time — do you cajole, threaten, plead, shout, beg, pray...?

A. Yes, I do all these things. As a Manager you have to do all these things. As a Manager I try to look at a match constructively because I only have a very short period of time to rectify mistakes. Most of the preparation goes on in the week before the match and then I sit during the first half and have only a few minutes at half time in which to get over clearly to the players what's on my mind. Sometimes I rant and rave, other times I have got to go in and feed them very positive information rather quickly.

Talking about half times, I remember very well the Sheffield Wednesday match. I would have loved to have got that goal on video. Anyway now they are top of the league and they come down here on a crest of the wave with a lot of support. If ever there was a pitch made for Sheffield Wednesday it was that one. They are a 'wacky' side and the pitch was covered in mud. It suited them perfectly; made for their style. They can whack the ball and turn the opposition round very quickly. Mind you we lost four balls that day with their big kicks!

Now we are a footballing side and after ten minutes or so they gave us all sorts of problems, had a near miss and then got a goal. Now we are still trying to play *our* way, and I thought to myself 'bloody hell!'

So I went in at half time knowing that our two touch passing was not made for the pitch and we are having problems, because now they are knocking big balls up the back for dropping, so with my back four against their two there were big gaps. So I went in and slated them. I told them we had to push up more from the back and play Curren off-side because he was going on early runs and because we were all back they could knock it up with an inch of our box. I said "If we let him go he's off-side and that will disrupt their rhythmn. Not only that, we are going to be more together as a team instead of being stretched out". I said "We are playing too much football (now I don't often say that) we have got to adapt more."

Now they went out and did very much what I asked them to do. We pushed up and Curren was caught off-side about four times. But they didn't do exactly what I told them. They didn't stop playing our type of football which I honestly didn't think they could do on that pitch. And they played magnificently. I went to them after and told them "you proved me wrong."

But the highlighting goal; and what a goal that was. It set off from Ron Hillyard's hands; it went all through the pitch before it was struck in the net. I think there must have been ten passes — a hell of a lot of movement involved — all on a pitch up to your ankles in mud.

Q. What do you think was your worst game at Gillingham?

A. As I have already told you I have a bad memory

for such things but I think the first was probably the worst. I took over on the Tuesday and we played at Aldershot on the Saturday. We lost 4-1, even though Ron saved a penalty that day. I remember the game very well and I was sitting on the bench with Bill Collins. I turned to him and said "do they always play as well as this Bill?" Yes, that game definitely sticks out.

Q. Any particularly good games you remember?
A. I don't know. There have been lots of enjoyable games. Perhaps early season last year the Luton game and then the Norwich match here but I don't remember very well. I tend to remember what happened not long ago but then again I remember winning at Crystal Palace and that was three years ago. Yes that really was a great game come to think about it.

But the season before last was really outstanding. When you think that we went through the season losing only eight of forty-six matches and getting fifty-nine points. The courage of the side was tremendous because we had injuries. We had Damien out for the last three months and John Crabbe out for the last two months but still we kept the team going. At the end we were picking the most peculiar sides what with injuries and suspensions! Garry Armstrong for example played in the mid field.

But they kept the thing going and towards the end I think the whole character of the side was shown when after we realised we couldn't go up we went to Chesterfield. People thought we were just going to go out and fulfil the fixture but we went out and beat them. That was really an outstanding season and it was sad to see at the end of the day that we didn't get promotion when normally, nine times out of ten, with the points we had we would have won it.

I remember well turning to Alan (Hodgkinson) and telling him that next year was going to be the hardest because everybody will be there looking for us instead of us coming along quietly as we had done that year and suddenly emerging.

Q. Do you have any superstitions or pre-match rituals?
A. I believe that if you work hard enough you should get your own just rewards, but of course you're always living on a knife's edge. There is so little between all the sides and the Third Division is no different. Injury or a new signing could just tilt the balance.

Q. How do you think a football club should be run?
A. Some people say that you should run a football club like a business. You should run it along business-like lines but you can't run it like a business, there are so many intangibles. Your star player breaks a leg and suddenly you are struggling. You haven't got a factory floor full of machines so that if one goes wrong you can easily replace it.

Q. How do you feel about this season?
A. I am looking forward to it very much. I don't want to talk about last year's disappointment or the year before's near miss. That's history. That's in the books. I always feel in the summer a sense of looking forward to next season and what's going to happen. The biggest 'look forward' for everybody here is to get in to the Second Division and we know it's going to take a lot of hard work and graft. Just look at the league and the teams and you know it's never going to get easier.

DAMIEN RICHARDSON, CLUB CAPTAIN 1979/80

Q. What do you think are the qualities necessary for a professional footballer?
A. The basic quality is skill, which incorporates ball control and passing ability. The higher the standards you play the better those qualities must be. Ball control must be instantaneous. Passing will be telepathic.

Temperament comes in later with a lot of other things. To be a good professional footballer you need temperament, honesty, character. A good professional doesn't say "I had a good game last Saturday so I will take it easy this Saturday."

A professional footballer is a consistent footballer.

Q. You mentioned honesty, but you can't really cheat in football can you?
A. Yes, they can cheat, but it's only when you're involved in the game that you know who is cheating. There are cheats in every facet of life. We are no different from the local Co-op in this respect. You have got to be honest with your team mates, coach, supporters and so on, but the first person you have got to be honest with is yourself. Some people don't even realise they are cheating. They take the easy way out and are really cheating themselves.

You see a win is so vitally important that you need to have eleven people committed to a cause. Without getting too technical I'll give you a couple of quick examples. An honest footballer will make a bad pass into a good pass. If I make a bad pass to him which is, say ten yards too far in front he will make the effort to get the ball without just turning and shrugging his shoulders. Another example is where a lad will make a mistake, possibly conceding a goal, and will not turn round and blame somebody else.

We are in this together. The honesty of putting yourself out to help a team mate who may be in trouble, and not just looking after yourself.

Q. What do you think of lucky charms or pre-match rituals?
A. It's important that you can get into a good frame of mind for a good match build up. This may entail rituals; I have known some really strange ones in my time. One player used to always take Vitamin C tablets at the exact time every Saturday. Then there are going different ways to the ground, different suits, sitting in a certain place for the pre-match lunch. All these types of things. It does no harm at all (as long as it's not too ridiculous). I knew one lad

who always put his shorts on last, as he was actually going up the steps to enter the pitch!

Q. If you are having a nightmare game how do you get out of it?
A. The best way of combating it is either to put up with it or make life as difficult as possible for the man you're playing directly against. My first game with Shamrock Rovers was a total disaster and I hated it. Then, however, I was very young. I was also inexperienced, and none of the other members of the team came to my help.

Later in my career, however, we were playing Shrewsbury. It was all going wrong. I told Terry Nicholl "Just forget about me — by-pass me, go straight to the two strikers." I intended working in my own little area making sure nothing would emanate from mistakes I would make but I would still be part of the side. This went on for about an hour then with twenty minutes to go I scored a goal — it turned out to be the winner. The point I am trying to make is that when it happened to me the first time with Shamrock Rovers I did not know how to cope with it. The second time I did.

DR. CLIFFORD SYDNEY GROSSMARK   CHAIRMAN

Q. When did you first start watching football?
A. The first football match I saw was with my Uncle who had a sister in Shepherds Bush; he took me to see Queens Park Rangers. They were playing Exeter City but I can't remember the exact date. I used to get a 6d cheap day return ticket to Tottenham as a boy and can remember the first game I saw there. It was on the 26th January 1926 when Tottenham played Manchester United in an F.A. Cup Tie and drew, two each. So I must have gone to Q.P.R. earlier than that.

Q. Can you tell me something about your background, when you first played football. Where you were born and so on?
A. I was born in the East End of London but moved at a very, very early age to Hendon, and Hendon is what I remember best. I went to an elementary school and from there won a scholarship to a grammar school; Central Foundation which is in the City of London. I played football for Central Foundation and also for St. Bartholomews Hospital. I left school in 1935 and qualified at St. Bartholomews in 1939. After that I did a few locums (supply work) and then came down to Chatham for eighteen months to do a locum here. It's lasted forty years.

Q. What was your first contact with Gillingham Football Club?
A. I was a season ticket holder in the post War Southern League days. Then in the early 1950's. Well, one day the Club doctor was in hospital and I took his place as the team doctor, at Archie Clark's request. It still remains a part of history, not because of my presence, but as a result of the team's 9-4 win over Exeter. In 1954, in the summer Archie Clark dispensed with the doctor and asked me to come to the Club. So I was the doctor in 1954 and I came on the Board in 1957 and sadly one of my first jobs, and it still hurts me to admit this, was to be involved with the removal of Archie Clark. Then in the early 1960's I was elected the Chairman. Since then I have been regularly elected to the Chair.

Q. What do you see as the job of a Club Chairman and do you think there are any special qualities needed for such a post?
A. I suppose that if I were to be a cheat and tell you lies (which I don't want to do) I would say that the Club Chairman's job was to see that everybody does their allocated part of the work. But in this Club, and again this would sound pompous, we have got two people doing the main work. I do the day to day work and Charles Cox does the fund raising. He's the optimist of the partnership and I am the very guarded pessimist. I spend my time reining him in! But please let me make it clear the Directors don't run the Club's office and administration. It would be far too presumptuous for me to suggest that. The day to day work in the office is handled very efficiently by Richard Dennison, our Secretary, and of course Gerry Summers has control of the team.

Regarding special qualities I suppose I am probably speaking against myself but having said that, I feel a good businessman, a good driver and a good delegator would be a better Chairman than myself because I am totally immersed in football lore and interested in the game of football. I can tell you who played outside left for Hartlepools last year, but that's not so important as what someone like the late George Wright would have been. 'He was a driver'. He came on the Board with young Charles Cox in 1960 and at one time wanted a 'run at the helm'. I think he would have been a very good Chairman because he was far more efficient than me even though he knew little about football; and he was a good businessman but sadly he died, in May 1975.

Q. What's the situation regarding the Board today?
A. There are now four of us. We have Brian Moore, who is an extremely useful man to us, and we have got Charles Cox and Joe Leech. He, Joe that is, came on in 1938 by virtue of something which is most amusing and I think may well be a part of your story. In 1938 we had Munich and there were twelve Directors who had got £400 guarantees. When Munich occurred, the Bank Manager called the guarantees in and the Club couldn't pay them. Joe

St Bartholomew's Hospital A.F.C. 1938-9.

Leech's father had just died and rather than pay the Estate the £400, which the Club were duty bound to do, they put Joe on the Board and he has been there ever since.

Q. The Manager of a First Division Club once said that the worst moments of his life were watching his team. He loved the job apart from that. What do you think?

A. What he said was true. I relish the thought of going to watch Chatham play. I like to see Internationals. I like to see non-events where I have no particular interest. I like to see twenty kids kicking a ball about in the Park. I am perfectly happy and interested in that, but the tension that develops in this 'dog eats dog' situation which is the Football League is very worrying.

A. What qualities do you think are necessary to be a good professional footballer?

A. I guess I am biased here because I haven't got them. I think it's extreme and absolute physical fitness. I like to think I had the skill when I was younger, but not the fitness. Whenever I played against boys who didn't have my skill but had the fitness they always beat me. Therefore I put physical fitness first and then absolute dedication.

Q. What have been your worst moments as Chairman of Gillingham?

A. My worst moments have been the two relegation escapes, one at Shrewsbury and one at Leyton Orient. They were in the Hayward years. The next year there was no doubt about it and we were relegated from Christmas onwards. That was no problem once I knew.

Q. In an interview with the Press you stated that when Ashurst left as Manager, it was the 'worst moment of my life'.

A. Oh yes, I naturally remember that. It was when Ashurst left hurriedly. Well, it was traumatic for me because there were certain 'spivs' here and they seized the opportunity to get themselves away. That's why it was traumatic, in the sense that I had to run the Club, and to be put in the position of a Manager as well for one or two weeks was most alarming.

Q. What about exhilarating moments. Are there any that stick in your mind?

A. I suppost the promotion at Newport in April 1964 with the George Francis goal and then promotion with Andy Nelson in 1974 with the Brian Yeo goal at Colchester.

Q. Any moments of great pride?
A. Being accepted in 1963 to the Third Division and Fourth Division Committee to the Football League. I became Chairman in 1968 and elected to the newly created vacancy on the League Management Committee in 1975.

Q. Do you have any pre-match rituals or habits during the games?
A. I sit in the same seat and I pray. I can't eat before a game. I have recently taken to having a brandy which has a disastrous effect because by 4.40 p.m. or 4.45 p.m. I have got to run somewhere and I am not always immediately available to entertain the visitors, especially after a defeat.

Q. As the Chairman you keep a very low profile? Few people have heard of you and hardly any would recognise you although you have been the driving force (even though you won't admit it) behind the Club for many years and done a lot to keep the Club going. Why is that?
A. The answer to that is very simple. I have found that Managers resent utterances from Directors. In the main they are right because Directors don't know very much about it and it is difficult to make utterances which are truthful without being critical. And I restrict my statements to one or two per annum, perhaps for a newspaper, New Year's message or the Annual Report. I just report factually without any hyperbole. In the modern vernacular, I prefer to retain 'a low profile' because I think that not to do so can cause all sorts of trouble. I respect the Sydney Wale approach at Tottenham.

Q. On the subject of Sydney Wale he once said that a Third Division Director has the worst job in the world, he takes all the kicks and back-biting, etc. Do you agree with this?
A. Yes I do. I have had recent experience of this because the cynics started their chanting again in the month of April, 1980! As a Director I must naturally give the Manager a complete and absolutely free hand. If I do then I am wrong and if I don't then I am wrong!

Q. The impression I got before interviewing you was that you were a person without humour, and yet, if I may say so, I am finding this conversation most entertaining. You do, however, look terribly worried during matches. Are you the worrying kind?
A. Yes, I worry, worry, worry all the time. I worry about looking at the asymmetrical Gordon Road Stands. Asymmetry is the bane of my life. For me it is an obsessional neurosis — perhaps it is one of the signs of madness — but if there is a book on the table and it isn't symmetrical then I cannot read it. The fact that I have to look at the Stand from the Directors' box worries me such a lot. I would desperately like to get the whole Stand in a straight line. I know for lots of people this is of no importance but it's all part of the image of the Club and I do so much want it to be right. And of course I worry about the finance, results, gates and the Club's image.

Q. What are your views on the future?
A. Well, I can answer that one quite simply. All I am concerned about is tomorrow. I have no ability to see the future. I just plan for tomorrow. I plan to keep the Club solvent. I want to see the Club built up.

RICHARD DENNISON, CLUB SECRETARY

Q. How did you first get involved in football?
A. My father was a football manager and when I was about sixteen I had trials with Chelsea as a goalkeeper. There were so many people trying to get in to professional football at the time and I didn't feel I wanted to find myself struggling to make ends meet in the Third or Fourth Division as a player who could, at the end of an apprenticeship find himself being told "Sorry son, you're not good enough." The only thing I wanted to do was to be involved with football but if it wasn't going to be out there on the pitch it had to be somewhere else. I left school and went to teach in a Prep School in Hampshire to try and give myself time to see if there would be any opportunities. At that time my father was at Coventry and obviously people got to know me there.

Coventry had just got into the First Division and the Secretary, Eddie Plumley, wanted someone to help as an assistant and I went there. I was there for eight-and-a-half years.

Q. What made you leave?
A. I couldn't see myself getting any further. Eddie Plumley was good at his job and only in his forties and so I began looking around. I was approached by

Port Vale and had two years there. They were the worst two years of my life in football. But perhaps that's being a bit unfair.

Q. How did you find yourself at Gillingham?
A. Gillingham asked Port Vale if they could talk to me with a view to coming here, and I eventually came in January 1978. It has been my most exciting and enjoyable time in that I am working with people whom I respect and who gave me faith in human nature again. For example the Chairman here is tremendous. A lot of people in these Towns don't know the Chairman, don't know him at all. They look upon him as an introverted gentleman who has nothing to do with them. In fact he is one of the most learned men in football and a genuine gentleman. I can't say any more than that.

Q. What's the role of a Secretary in a Club?
A. The basic involvement of a Secretary is to run the clerical side of the job. The Manager runs the team at this Club, and I run the other side of it. The paperwork that's involved when signing players, putting on matches, involving people in sponsorships and so on. The Manager will say "I want this done" and then hand it over to me to deal with. For example I have in front of me now forms which have to be sent in for us to retain the contracts of people at the Club for a further period of time. That sort of thing.

Basically the Secretary has to deal with everything outside of playing. The Manager is solely in charge of everything that involves the team in any way at all and the Secretary here at this Club is in charge of the paperwork for everything else.

Q. By the way, what did you teach at Prep School — football?
A. Quite amusingly I taught English, French and Geography and that was quite an education in itself. I don't know if you know much about English Prep Schools but if they can find somebody who is young and who is not totally stupid then they will take you on for your sporting ability and say "Would you mind Monday to Friday between 9 and 12 doing some teaching? In the afternoons I would teach sports.

ALAN HODGKINSON, DEPUTY MANAGER

... with Dean White.

Q. What do you see as the qualities necessary for a good player?
A. Attitude, dedication and discipline. By attitude I mean a thirst for hard work to better yourself, a desire to want to play, to want to do one's job and a need to win, a will to win in fact. By discipline I mean self-discipline. To control your body, to discipline yourself to fitness. To take care of your body, going to bed early, not smoking and so on.

Q. You allege you are twenty-nine and a bit. How big is the bit?
A. No comment.

Q. Did you go straight to football from school?
A. After leaving school I worked for a butchers. There were no apprentices in those days so I played for the local youth side and signed professional at 17 for Sheffield United. I did have hopes of becoming a concert pianist when young. My father and elder brother would play in concerts and my father always hoped that I would take it up professionally. Unfortunately for him I was far more interested in football and would skip piano lessons to play in the park. I still do 'tinkle the ivories' a little bit.

Q. Tell me something about your football career?
A. Well, between 1954 and 1972 I notched up five hundred and fifty-two League games and had the opportunity of playing for England with such players as Stanley Matthews and Tom Finney, Billy Wright and Nat Lofthouse. That was in the fifties. In the sixties I played with people like Bobby Charlton, Jimmy Greaves and Duncan Edwards so when people try and compare Stanley Matthews with Georgie Best I can say I had the opportunity of playing against them both. I retired in 1971 from professional football and went to the staff of Sheffield United, as a coach. When Gerry came to Gillingham he asked me to come with him. It was a big wrench leaving a Club after so long (I had spent half my working life there). However, I have never regretted it.

Q. How do you motivate people?

A. You motivate people by results really. The sooner you get a sequence of results going for you that's motivation. As soon as the last game is finished and you have won it you cannot wait for the next game. That is motivation.

Q. Are you an emotional person where football is concerned?

A. I am a very emotional watcher of the game. I get extremely disappointed if, for example, we play very well and get beaten in the last minute. I also get emotional if the team plays badly. I get uptight about critics and also about cynics but I suppose that's football. They are all welcome really. If the boot boys, critics, cheer leaders and so on left, there would be no football.

Q. Do you think coaching is important?

A. The coaching here is really done by Gerry Summers, he is the head man but we all help out. Yes, I do think coaching has played a big part in modern football and for the better I feel. That's the technical coach I am talking about. In my day all you had really was a physical education instructor getting you to run around the pitch. Times changed after the Hungarians visited us in 1953. They came with two centre halfs and attacking full backs. Four in the middle of the park and two up the front. It was tremendous. They were the people who changed the structure of football when they defeated England 6-3 at Wembley in the November. It shook British Football to the core, not only because it was England's first ever home defeat by a continental side, but because of the immaculate display of the Hungarians which proved how far the old masters had slipped behind. In May 1954 they gave England an even bigger beating winning 7-1 in Budapest. Things then began to change in English Football and I think for the better.

Q. What interests have you got outside football?

A. None really, football people are my kind of people. I get on well with football people.

Q. How do you feel about aggression on the pitch?

A. I think what people do not realise, and especially Referees, is that we work in the fresh air from Monday until Saturday afternoon - six days a week. We have physical contact. Competitive physical contact with each other. We are different animals to anyone else in the world I would think. Our approach is naturally aggressive. We are different people and react differently to people who sit in offices. Most referees sit in offices. Referees may be sales representatives driving in a car all week and they forget that we are automatically aggressive. They try to make it a non-physical game. A non-bodily contact game. If this happens the game is gone. You are getting silly bookings because the referees do not know the difference between a competitive player and a dirty player.

JOE LEECH – DIRECTOR

Q. You have been involved now with the Club for over forty years. During that time are there any moments that stick in your memory?

A. That's a difficult question, there have been so many. I remember vividly standing and watching the team when I was a youngster. I didn't like the idea of sitting because I enjoyed the banter with other members of the crowd. I liked to stand in the middle, right on the half way line. However, when I started courting, somehow I felt it would be wrong to make my girlfriend stand with me so I started sitting in the Directors' Box with my father.

One moment of immense joy for me was when we were re-admitted to the Football League. That was certainly a great moment. We had been working years to get back there.

Q. You joined the Board of Directors in 1937/38, the year the team were relegated. My research indicates quite a lot of financial problems in the 'old' days.

A. Oh dear yes. Every year we used to have a terrific overdraft. We would have to start the season scraping the bottom of the barrel because the Bank Manager would say we could have no more money. Then we would have to sit down and try to do our sums and see how much money we could get for the next two or three gates and so on. Then we would go to the Bank Manager and try and arrange accommodation; to tell him the 'bright side' of the position. I can remember when my father would take the team away. I would go with him as a school boy and when we met the team Secretary at Gillingham Station the first thing the Secretary would ask for was money for the fares. And this happened every time!

Q. Are there any particular players who stick in your mind over the years at Gillingham?

A. Yes, Hughie Russell. He was an all round player and certainly sticks in my mind.

Q. How do you see yourself as a Director?

A. When I was younger I was much more active. I became intensely interested and have remained so but now I think of myself as a professional looker. We had some great fun in the old days especially canvassing in the League Clubs to obtain our re-entry into the Football League. I think I visited about three-quarters of the League Clubs at the time. Charlie Cox, that's the old Charlie Cox, organised spectaculars at the Annual Meeting of the Football League and so on. They were really terrific times. Now of course I am older I sit back much more.

Q. What was the change round like once you moved into the Football League?

A. When we were in the Southern League and the Kent League, we had a very good team. We won everything, Kent Cup, Southern League Cup, Kent Senior Cup and at the same time had a team of part-timers. We made money then. That was very exciting. We made money and we also spent a lot of money on having the ground levelled, concrete terracing built, stand extended, painting, building turnstiles and so on. Also we paid off a lot of our old debts.

As soon as we got back into the Football League then we got into debt again. You see, during the War school kids were becoming adults, eighteen, nineteen-year-olds and so on. And they had never known any entertainment because of the War years. Very little entertainment at all. At the time we were getting anything from 16,000 to 18,000 gates over at Gillingham and of course we had a part-time team. Once we got into the Football League we had a full-time team which almost trebled our wage bill plus the fact that enthusiasm began to wane a little. As we were not terribly successful in the League after two or three seasons we were back to square one, with gates of about 4,000 or 5,000 and £20,000 overdrawn! Still, that's in the old days. Times are much better now.

Q. You are a very jovial character, Mr Leech. How do you cope with criticism of the Club?

A. I enjoy it when people say to me in the street either "Well done" or "Get lost". I am interested in the team and I know they are interested in the team. In a football club there are always bones of contention. It's one of the facts of football. I remember on one occasion when I was Vice-Chairman, I was down at a builders' firm behind Rochester Station and wandering along the river. There was a ship unloading wood pulp in bales into the lighters and there were lots of stevedores there. As I walked a voice floated across the Medway, "You wanna sack the bloody Manager". I had to laugh to myself. That sort of thing always happens in football.

Q. What's your philosophy?

A. I am an optimist. I am optimistic about the future. You have to be or you would not stick it!

BRIAN MOORE, DIRECTOR

Interview after League Cup game with Blackburn, 3rd September, 1980.

Q. How did you feel up there this evening?

A. I think it's more difficult watching a game like that then it is doing a live game on T.V. on a Saturday night. I feel more tension there than at any other time I think. At the end of the game it's like a Cup-Tie you know, your stomach is like a big concrete ball inside. It weighs very heavily; and I think it's the same for all directors. You know, directors get tarred as being people with nice fat stomachs and gold watch chains, who come along for the whisky and the easy ride, but in my experience most directors are people (particularly in the smaller clubs) who really work very hard for their clubs. The Third and Fourth Divisions are littered with people who maybe turn their backs on their jobs more than they should in order to put more time into a club. A prime example of this is our Chairman, Dr. Grossmark, who is an excellent medical man but whose practice I think would flourish a hell of a lot more if he were not giving so much of his time every day of the week and every week of the year to Gillingham Football.

Q. Do you ever get excited up there? Do you shout at all?

A. I never shout in the Box. I always used to when I was on the terraces but I never shout in the Box. Joe Mercer used to say a terrific thing when he was Manager of Aston Villa and they were having a bad time. He would sit next to his Chairman and the Chairman said to him, "Joe, I don't know how it is you can't shout through the course of a game." Joe replied, "It's a bit like a dog swimming across a lake; it looks nice and serene, but underneath by God there's some activity going on." And that's exactly the same for me. You sit there and try not to show your feelings but my God when that Blackburn equaliser went in five minutes from the end tonight then you feel like . . .
Q. How long have you been watching Gillingham?
A. I first watched them immediately after the war in 1946.
Q. Are you a local?
A. No, my mother was born here in Britton Street but I was born and brought up in the Weald of Kent and I went to school at Cranbrook which is a Public School and meant that we had to go to school on Saturdays. I used to play truant in my schoolboy days to come and watch big Cup-Ties here. I remember coming to watch Orient play in the Cup-Tie when Gillingham was still in the Southern League and I was first in the queue down at the Town end of the ground on the day Queens Park Rangers came in 1948 when the ground record of 23,002 was set. I came up on the first bus from the village and I was queuing at half past nine.
Q. So you could really be called one of the 'lunatic' supporters?
A. I am certainly a very keen supporter and have been, as I say, from 1946 onwards when they played in the Southern League and when they got 10,000 crowds at every game. Up behind the Town End there was no terrace, it was just an ash tip and you would stand there and your toes were pushing their way through the tops of your shoes by the time the afternoon was finished!
Q. Did you have the same place each week?
A. I used to stand in fact just over by the Gordon Road Stand. I could go to exactly the spot where I stood every game I came to, and I remember the players like Hughie Russell and Jackie Briggs and George Forrester.
Q. Who were the best players do you think you saw? The ones that stick out the most?
A. Well, you see, I think in the same way that you never lose your first love when it comes to supporting a team (that's why people say to me "Why do you support Gillingham?". It's because it was the first team that I supported and you always have a soft spot for them) and I think distance always lend enchantment with the players. There were two players who I shall always remember, one was Hughie Russell, the Centre Forward in the late forties who was a magnificent header of the ball and really elegant and terrific goal scorer. And in the number eight shirt was 'Tug' Wilson who was a great little worker and was always in the thick of things. A terrific little player. One of my schoolboy thrills was on top of a bus going down the High Street after a Southern League game and Tug Wilson came up the stairs and sat alongside me. You can imagine my feelings. These days players have limousines and so on, but Tug used to come to and from a game on a bus up the High Street!
Q. Then you were on the terraces, now you are in the Directors' Box; do you see a vast difference, a different atmosphere, etc?
A. It's a more restrained atmosphere in the Directors' Box although the feelings are exactly the same. But there is a code of honour, if you like, where you are not supposed to shout and jump up and down, although you do get to your feet (it's inevitable) when a goal is scored and so on, and at the moment when you have won. But then you have to restrain yourself and be very polite to the opposition and say "Very sorry, your blokes played very well indeed. . ." and so on but inside the feeling is exactly the same.
Q. Do you have any superstitions, anything you do before a match game?
A. I am a superstitious person and a country boy. There is an old saying about magpies, the birds, 'one for sorrow, two for joy, three for a girl, four for a boy', so if I see a single magpie on the way to Gillingham Football Club I move heaven and earth and look around to see a second one — two for joy!
Q. Have you any bad moments in football?
A. I think the worst moment, as a Director, was a Boxing Day here about two or three years ago when the side had been playing well, up to Christmas and then it faltered very badly. Crystal Palace came down here Boxing Day and beat us 3 or 4 and they murdered us. It was a miserable way to spend Christmas but the thing that really upset me was that, although the side had played well, giving terrific entertainment (there's no doubt about that), suddenly the crowd around us turned on the Chairman and Gerry Summers which I thought a very uncharitable thing to do, to be honest with you, and a very unseasonable thing to do at that time. I am a great believer that once you take your first shilling from the public then you turn away any right to worry about criticism but it did seem to me unfair that the Gillingham fans went for the Chairman and Gerry Summers at that particular moment, particularly after what had been a good season.
Q. You obviously know more about football than most people in the country. What would you say makes a good player. A good professional player?
A. I think there are so many qualities a player needs

and one of course is pure skill. You can't get anywhere unless you have got skill. I think a lot of things can be grafted onto it and to a certain extent players can be manufactured. Keegan is a prime example of that and I think he will be the first to say he is by no means the most skilful player in the Country but by dedication and tremendous hard work and enthusiasm he's built onto the skill he has got. So I think two things must cross fertilise if you like. You have got to have great skill but you have equally got to have great dedication. And a good degree of courage as well — physical courage.

Q. Are you born with skill or do you learn this?
A. No, I think you are born with it but I think that with dedication certain things can be, as it were, added to this. But skill is the first thing that is required.

Q. Can you remember any moments of great elation as a Director and also as a fan?
A. The greatest moment for me, on the terraces, was in fact that day back in '48 when we drew 1-1 here with Queens Park Rangers. That to me is a day I shall always remember no matter how long I support Gillingham. I mean they were a hell of a good Third Division South Side. They were very good. A good professional outfit and they came down here and drew 1-1. Hughie Russell scored that day in fact for Gillingham.

My best moment in the Directors' Box? Well, it sounds pretty mundane, but I think at the same time it illustrates the tension there is. The very first away game that I went to as a Director was to Southend United when Southend were having a terrific spell near the top of the Third Division. It was some time in November and a night game. It would have been in 1974 or 1975 and we were, if not at the bottom, very close. I think we were the bottom Club and they were nearly at the top and we were in desperate trouble. We went to Southend and we drew 2-2 and I remember it was the first time I had ever sat next to the Chairman who also never wants to share his feelings and remains absolutely tranquil (it appears) throughout a game. Well the tension in those last four or five minutes, as we were hanging on for 2-2 was unbelievable and as the final whistle went he said "We've done it! We've done it! We've done it!" and I went to the Directors' Room and I remember it took ten minutes before I could safely hold a cup of tea without slopping it all with my shaking hands. People say "What's your greatest moment as a Director" and then say "Maybe it's a Cup-Tie or something" but it wasn't. It was a cold November night at Southend when we drew 2-2.

Q. You must have seen thousands of football matches, the best teams and the worst all over the world and yet you still have this affinity with the Club?
A. I think in a way I am a fraud, to be honest with you. Perhaps not quite a fraud but I am not as close to the Club as I would like to be simply on the basis that I live a crazy existence in my working life. I never know where I am going to be. That may sound flash but it's not meant to be. It's just that my work load is pretty enormous at the moment and I live near Orpington, so it is thirty or thirty-five miles away from the Club so really all I can do is to get here for Board Meetings and for mid-week games; go away for mid-week games and be on the end of a telephone if the Chairman wants to talk to me — and we talk maybe three or four times a week at some length. But I feel slightly frustrated by that, because it's such a terrific little Club. What I would really like is a nice close association with it, and when eventually I grow a grey old beard and retire, it will be nice to know that on Saturdays, and week days, I can toddle off down here and maybe contribute a little more.

Q. Charlie Cox is an optimist. Dr Grossmark is a pessimist; what are you?
A. I am a catalyst! A balance between both. I listen with respect to both of them, but with slight amusement. When I go on the 'phone to Charlie I say "We are going to win the Cup again, Charlie, are we" and when I go on to the Doc I always say "Were we really as bad as you think we were, Doc?"

WILLIAM COLLINS, YOUTH TEAM MANAGER

... with Danny Westwood.

Q. I know that everyone tends to work together at Gillingham, but your main responsibility is the Youth Team. When you are watching boys playing and trying to decide whether they have a future in the game what exactly do you look for?

A. The first thing you look for in a schoolboy is ability. Ability to play; his control, vision, passing of the ball. 'Ability' is hard to define but we know it when we see it because we've been doing the job for so many years. The next thing, which I suppose is the most important of all in the long run, is character. Without character and attitude, if you have all the skill in the world you will never be a success, you'll always be strumming along from Club to Club. In fact attitude is more important sometimes than ability but of course if you got the two together then you really have got some player.

Q. What advice would you give to someone who wants to play football?

A. That they have got a lot of hard work in front of them. They haven't got it made just because they become apprentices. We try and give them good habits and we do it successfully. All the people who have been through this Club have got good habits. They know what the game is about and they will be a credit to whatever Club they finish up playing for and I think it is because we start with them early. We all look upon this as very important at Gillingham. None of the apprentices who have come here go away without a sense of values. They never give officials problems because that's the first thing they learn. If a player argues with an official he is not paying attention to what he should be doing on the field and that's no good for his pals who play with him or the club he plays for.

Q. How did you get involved with football?

A. I started when I was a kid at school. Before I was six I remember I was practising with a tennis ball up against the school wall and I was making so much noise that my Headmaster took me in and stood me on his chair until lunchtime. My mother was going crazy because she didn't know where I had gone. The first team I played for was the Boys' Brigade and then during the War I played in wartime football moving on eventually to my first professional Club, Distillery, then Linfield and Belfast Celtic. But football was in my family as my father was an amateur international. I came across to Luton on a month's trial and then to Gillingham.

Q. Tell me something about the Gillingham Youth policy?

A. I had been involved in Gillingham's administration before but when Freddie Cox was here he asked me to come back to Gillingham to start the Youth Scheme, this was during the sixties, and I have been here ever since. Naturally I have lots of contacts in the area. The eleven to fourteen-year-olds play for their own Sunday teams and of course their school teams. A lot of them play at County and District level and we keep an eye on them and I am in turn told by various people, sportsmasters and so on about particular boys. We all go and watch the games from time to time and have our own team of scouts within the Club. I use the word 'We' because Gerry, Alan and John are all involved in this. So when we hear of a particular boy from one of our scouts or contacts, or in turn see them ourselves, we will go and watch the lad and if he is good enough have him along here for a year playing in practice games and then if they are good enough they stay on. We are becoming very selective these days and only take those who we feel have a genuine chance of succeeding.

Q. How do you deal with the social welfare of the younger players?

A. The person in charge of them, when they are very young, has got most to do with them and should teach them good habits on and off the field. On this line the groundwork is laid at home. Some people are easier to deal with than others and we have come across one or two right handfuls here, but at the end of their apprenticeship they will turn out o.k. Their social welfare, if they are living away from home, is important to us and we make sure that their 'digs' are good. We know all the landladies personally and know that the lads will get good food and that they will be looked after like a member of the family.

JOHN SHORT, CHIEF SCOUT

Q. How long have you been in football?
A. All in all it must be forty-three years now. I started in 1937 when I was about sixteen going firstly to Leeds as a boy, which in those days meant a boot cleaner and a sweeper of the stands and so on. There were no apprentices then. When the War came along I guested for Newcastle and Hartlepools and after the War I moved to Millwall and stayed there from 1948 to 1957 playing as a wing half. From there I went to Huddersfield as Chief Coach moving to Sheffield.

Q. Are there any moments that stick out in your playing career?
A. I remember playing against Middlesborough once when there were about eight minutes to go and we were losing 3-0. We finished drawing 3-3 and I scored the equaliser in the last minute! That was when I was playing for Leeds. Another time was when I was at Millwall and we played against Manchester United in the Fourth Round of the Cup. We lost 1-0 but played ever so well and it was unfortunate; we should never have lost, but that's the way it goes.

Q. Did you like football?
A. I wouldn't change my football life even now.

Q. You came to Gillingham about two years ago after spending 17 years with Sheffield United. You are now the Chief Scout here, could you tell me something about what you do?
A. The first thing a scout has got to know, in fact got to have at his finger tips, is details of the players who are available. He has also got to know most of the players in the game and that includes both First, Second, Third and Fourth Division players because you never know! And to do that you have got to have contacts, in different places obviously. We have scouts in various parts of the Country, the North East, Midlands, Yorkshire and so on. They call me from time to time or if there is anything special I call them. They have got an area to cope with or to look at, and they work in that area. I cover the whole Country but Bill Collins does most of the local work (especially with the schoolboys). I suppose I drive about 35,000 miles a year to see players.

Q. What do you look for in a player?
A. He has got to have the skill first then he has got to have the temperament with the aggression. I don't mean aggressive, aggression. By aggression I mean he has got to be able to go and win the ball. But he has got to have the attitude to play. Dedication I suppose. He must have a desire to win. Really I suppose attitude is another word for dedication. We use both words. If a boy is say 21, 22 or 23 and if he is still willing to go and enjoy his game in whatever league he is playing in then that's attitude.

Q. Do you make an immediate decision — I mean how do you KNOW that he is the right player for you?
A. It's like your job or any other, when you have been in it for long enough you do KNOW, but it depends. Sometimes when the game is finished it's either 'Yes' or 'No' immediately. Sometimes you can see what you are looking for. If someone is promising I will say 'I like so and so' and Gerry will go and have a look as well because he is the man that makes the decisions.

Q. Any moments that stick out in your scouting career?
A. Oh, that's a difficult one, you see in a job like this it takes three or four years before you can see the full fruits of your work.

Q. But are there any particular players that you can tell me about?
A. Micky Adams. He was one I got from Sheffield. I signed him as a schoolboy when I was at Sheffield then there was a change of Managers and the new Manager didn't fancy Mick when he left school so I said 'We'll have him down here' and we liked what we saw and he signed professional. It's things like this that make it worth while.

Q. You are also the physiotherapist are you not?
A. Yes, When I was at Millwall I used to coach and

do the injuries as well. When I left Sheffield I wasn't bothered about the injury side but when I came here we were looking for a physiotherapist as well because the person who used to do it had left. I therefore began to study physiotherapy and now do that. I suppose I always had an interest in it because I had to stop football as a result of osteo-arthritis in my knee. I played football for seventeen years and in those days you had to play when you shouldn't really have played. If you didn't play you lost your place in the team. Also they didn't have the know-how to get injuries right as they do these days. It used to be hot and cold water!

Q. Did you ever have any bad moments?
A. Yes, many times. I was just saying last night, coming back in the car, that my worst moment is on a Saturday. I have been to a game and might, or might not have got the half time score for Gillingham on the radio. Sometimes you know it's better not to get it at all! Well, coming back in the car it's terrible when you don't know the full result and thousands of others do. That's really a bad moment. If I hear we have lost I just can't be bothered listening anymore. They, I suppose, are my worst moments in the game.
Q. You seem to have a placid personality. Do you get excited at games?
A. When I watch other games I am neutral, but when I am watching Gillingham, although I don't shout or bawl, I get very worked up inside!

CHARLES COX VICE CHAIRMAN

Interview prior to League Cup game against Blackburn, 3rd September, 1980.

Q. What are your feelings at this moment?
A. Quite happy. With just a shade of the run of the green we shall win tonight!
Q. Dr. Grossmark told me you were the optimist?
A. Yes, that is quite true I suppose, I am a reasonably outgoing sort of person, things can't all be bad. Somewhere along the line the sun has got to shine as it has proved here I think. I don't think that we have sat still; we have got the ground 'half straight' and we are going to build the squash courts then we are going to build the stand in Gordon Road. So it can't all be wrong can it? We have raised something like half a million pounds in two years on ancillary things — nothing to do with football — so we must be as good as anybody in the League.
Q. So why do you think Dr. Grossmark worries?
A. Because I think Dr. Grossmark is a perfectionist and if he were a Director of Liverpool he would be just the same and quite honestly if we had what he basically wanted we would be a Liverpool! But let's remember that we are in the Third Division, although we want to get into the Second Division without a shadow of doubt.
Q. Dr. Grossmark said about you, in a light-hearted moment, when I asked him what was his main job here "I suppose to keep Charlie in check!"
A. That's fair comment!
Q. How did you get involved with Gillingham. Did you play football?
A. No, in fact I played rugby, but as you know my father was the Chairman here. And the interest was there. I have been coming to Gillingham since about Jack Knight's days, that must be about thirty odd years. I have been a Director here for twenty odd years.
Q. Do you have any superstitions?
A. Yes, little things like that. I believe in certain things. I don't know whether I am right or wrong — a load of hay today is luck all day!
Q. I mean you don't think that tonight's luck has been dispelled by Richard Dennison just this minute walking in and knocking over two hundred programmes!
A. Not in the least!
Q. You have been watching for thirty years and been a Director for twenty years, are there any players who stick out in your mind?

A. There were really lots of good players. Hughie Russell, Tug Wilson, Tommy Kingsnorth.

Q. Who was the best of the bunch, do you think?

A. Derek Lewis, I suppose, who went to Preston. But there were so many of them, it's so difficult. When you think of the Jimmy Boswells of this world — a lot of good players, a lot of really good players, it's a pity we did not have the pick of them for one game.

Q. What do you think, personally I mean, about what makes a good player — that's apart from the obvious need for skill?

A. Dedication — lots of dedication and wanting to play the game and I think we are coming into an era when footballers are coming into their own — Hard Times! But I think the system is completely up the wall.

Q. In what way —

A. It's completely up the wall when you start talking about the Keegans of this world — wonderful footballers, but I believe that to try and get a young kid to take his place in football and do it the right way when you have got the Keegans earning fortunes out of the game is difficult. There is a comfortable living for everyone to be earned really, but you know we have gone mad. Half the people are going to be out of work because the wage structure is so great you just cannot afford to pay the wages. Everybody is going to cut down to their bare minimum for example, fourteen or fifteen in a team and the others are going to be out of work!

Q. You believe that there are players who could be termed 'natural'. If such a player came to the Club what do you think the Club should teach him?

A. Not to be greedy and take it as it comes; I feel there is a tremendous amount of scope for the kids. You know that the kids are our lifeline really but I think if you honestly want to teach a kid something — if he has got something already then obviously you improve his skills — teach him not to be greedy and take it in his course and he will be a terrific player.

Q. When you are watching the players on the pitch do you have any emotions at all?

A. Do I? Do I? I swear at them! I get very, very excited; I holler and I shout and if they make a bad pass I am quick to shout "Damien for Christ's sake put the bloody thing where it ought to be!"

Q. What ideas do you have about football, improving it and so on?

A. We have all got different ideas about football. Your ideas won't be the same as mine. I think, for instance, that Billy Hughes is possibly the best footballer on our pitch. Other people turn round and say "He's a lazy little sod", he doesn't do this, he won't do that and so on. But nonetheless for that, my bone of contention is he is a good player.

Now we will go away to see a match and in the car coming home — from Blackburn there is a five hour drive home afterwards — the Doctor, Richard and myself and possibly another, tear the game to pieces. And the Doctor has rebuilt that team completely. He has got Smith, Keegan, you know, and at the end of the day I turn round and I say "Look Doc, we have got what we have got and if we don't like what we have got then let's find something better." This is where we don't agree. You see in Gerry's span of lifetime here — he has been here for five years now — I think Gerry has bought nineteen or twenty players. Now my bone of contention is that we should have bought two or three really top class players, in other words we should have bought Hollins and people of that calibre to go into the side to bring the kids on. That's the way I look at it. We don't argue about it, there is no fighting going on, no backbiting about it, just a difference of opinion. I am not here for very long, as you know I am fifty-two years of age and before I 'pop off' this mortal coil there is quite a lot to be done at Gillingham Football Club. The stand at Gordon Road has got to be completed before I shuffle off and we have got to be in the Second Division. Now I don't care how I do it or who I tread on to get it.

Q. How do you feel when you are walking along the street and somebody says something like, "Why don't you get your team in order."

A. I smile. Nobody gets more of that than I do. As you know my business is catering and I stand behind the counter and serve every cup of tea which is served at the Kent County Cricket Club. And everybody who comes around that counter knows that I am the Vice-Chairman of Gillingham Football Club. And everybody throws the dirt or they do the other thing whatever the case may be, and I talk about it and discuss it. I don't laugh it off because a lot of what the general public say is right, let's be truthful about it. They also pay the money! So they are entitled to say something aren't they?

My life at home is very tense by virtue of the fact of Gillingham Football Club. I spend a lot of time here. Gillingham Football Club is a love of mine. It is something very important in my life. I've told you what's important in my life, the Second Division and that Gordon Road stand.

In my view the prospects of this Football Club rely on the looks of the Football Club and the outlooks of the Football Club. If for example Blackburn come here tonight, look around and think to themselves what a dump that is no compliment to us is it? I mean you go to Blackburn and it is magnificent. Beautiful old Board Room and magnificent old stands.

Q. Do you ever get an urge to get onto the pitch or go down the dressing room?

A. No, we pay somebody else to do that. If he can't

do it we should get someone else. Sometimes I get an urge to tell them at a given time what, in my humble opinion, they did wrong but I think they know their bloody selves when they have done it.

Q. How do you feel about fans generally? Do you like the fans?

A. I am completely the reverse of Dr. Grossmark; he can watch with the gates shut. With nobody here. Now I am the reverse. I want thirty thousand people here. I want them all to come, I want the game to be good. I want everybody to enjoy it, and then go away and be ambassadors for this Football Club.

Q. The difference in personalities between you and Dr. Grossmark is quite amazing, but there is a sort of symbiosis.

A. Yes, we are two opposites.

He is very, very cautious and very, very wary. We are all that way a bit I suppose, but in his case if you have been smacked in the mouth a few times (and he has), then you do become cautious. It doesn't worry me.

I want to see this Club in the Second Division. I want to make this Club as nice as any Football Club we go to. You can see that by what we have done with the Office and what we are going to do with the squash courts, it now looks as fair as any in the Third Division.

I have told you about our aspirations but this can't be done without them (the fans). Without them coming through the turnstiles. Because to try and improve this thing it has got to be done through money which comes through the turnstiles. This Club costs about a thousand pounds in excess per week of what comes through the turnstiles. Now we have done a lot by raising money but without that person coming through the bloody turnstiles we can do nothing. If you want us to stay at square one then don't come. Criticise by all means. Because nobody is perfect. We could go out there tonight and play like a lot of idiots and lose 5-0. All right, so that's wrong, something's wrong but don't keep running it down, come again next week and have another go.

Q. Are there any moments in your life as a Director of Gillingham Football Club which have been terrible, I mean really terrible?

A. No, all wonderful, all just wonderful. All wonderful moments.

FROM THE RECORD BOOK

First Team Honours

Champions, Football League Division Four	1963 - 64
Runners-up, Football League Division Four	1973 - 74
Champions, Southern League	1946 - 47, 1948 - 49
Runners-up, Southern League	1947 - 48
Champions, Southern League Division Two	1894 - 95
Winners, Southern League Cup	1946 - 47
Champions, Kent League	1944 - 45, 1945 - 46

F. A. Cup
Best season — 5th Round — 1969 - 70

Football League Cup
Best season — 4th Round — 1963 - 64

Record Victories
Football League   : 9 - 4 v Exeter City, 6 January 1951
F. A. Cup   : 10 - 1 v Gorleston, 16 November 1957
Southern League   : 12 - 1 v Gloucester City, 9 November 1946

Record Defeats
Football League   : 2 - 9 v Nottingham Forest, 18 November 1950
                     4 - 9 v Bristol City, 15 January 1927
                     0 - 8 v Luton Town, 13 April 1929

Most Points
Football League   : 62, Division Four, 1973 - 74
Southern League   : 64, Division One, 1938 - 39
Kent League   : 37, Division One, 1945 - 46

Most Goals
Football League   : 90, Division Four, 1973 - 74
Southern League   : 106, Division One, 1938 - 39
Kent League   : 111, Division One, 1945 - 46

Record Goalscorers
Football League   : 31, Ernie Morgan, Division 3(S), 1954 - 55
                    31, Brian Yeo, Division Four, 1973 - 74
Southern League   : 35, Hughie Russell, Division One, 1948 - 49
Kent League   : 27, Vic Hole, Division One, 1945 - 46

Most League Goals in total aggregate
Brian Yeo scored 136 goals from 1963 to 1975

Most League appearances
John Simpson made 571 appearances between 1957 and 1972

Capped Players
Damien Richardson, 2 for Eire (1972 - 73 and 1979 - 80)
Freddie Fox, 1 for England (1924 - 25)

Record Attendances
Football League : 20,128 v Millwall   2 September 1950
F. A. Cup   : 23,002 v Q.P.R.   10 January 1948
F. L. Cup   : 20,566 v Arsenal   21 September 1966

Record Receipts
£14,203 v Shrewsbury Town (Division Three) 28 April 1979

Record Transfer Fee Received
£70,000 from Charlton Athletic for Dick Tydeman, December 1976

Record Transfer Fee Paid
£60,000 to Oxford United for Colin Duncan, January 1980

SEASON	POSITION	P	W	D	L	F	A	Pts
Southern League Division Two								
1894 - 95	1	12	11	0	1	57	10	22
Southern League Division One								
1895 - 96	6	18	7	4	7	30	37	18
1896 - 97	8	20	7	2	11	32	42	16
1897 - 98	6	22	9	4	9	37	37	22
1898 - 99	6	24	10	5	9	38	30	25
1899 - 1900	11	28	9	6	13	39	49	24
1900 - 01	12	28	7	5	16	34	51	19
1901 - 02	10	30	10	7	13	39	38	27
1902 - 03	6	30	11	11	8	37	35	33
1903 - 04	16	34	6	13	15	26	43	25
1904 - 05	9	34	11	11	12	40	40	33
1905 - 06	17	34	7	8	19	20	62	22
1906 - 07	16	38	12	9	17	47	59	33
1907 - 08	20	38	9	7	22	44	75	25
1908 - 09	7	40	17	7	16	48	59	41
1909 - 10	12	42	19	5	18	76	74	43
1910 - 11	18	38	11	8	19	34	65	30
1911 - 12	18	38	11	9	18	35	72	31
1912 - 13	15	38	12	10	16	36	53	34
1913 - 14	13	38	13	9	16	48	49	35
1914 - 15	20	38	6	8	24	43	82	20
World War I								
1915 - 1919	League Competition suspended							

SEASON	POSITION	P	W	D	L	F	A	Pts	
Southern League Division One									
1919 - 20	22	42	10	7	25	34	74	27	
Football League Division 3									
1920 - 21	22	42	8	12	22	34	74	28	*
Football League Division 3 (South)									
1921 - 22	18	42	14	8	20	47	60	36	
1922 - 23	16	42	15	7	20	51	59	37	
1923 - 24	15	42	12	13	17	43	58	37	
1924 - 25	13	42	13	14	15	35	44	40	
1925 - 26	11	42	17	8	17	53	49	42	
1926 - 27	20	42	11	10	21	54	72	32	
1927 - 28	16	42	13	11	18	62	81	37	
1928 - 29	22	42	10	9	23	43	83	29	*
1929 - 30	21	42	11	8	23	51	80	30	*
1930 - 31	16	42	14	10	18	61	76	38	
1931 - 32	21	42	10	8	24	40	82	28	*
1932 - 33	7	42	18	8	16	72	61	44	
1933 - 34	17	42	11	11	20	75	96	33	
1934 - 35	20	42	11	13	18	55	75	35	
1935 - 36	16	42	14	9	19	66	77	37	
1936 - 37	11	42	18	8	16	52	66	44	
1937 - 38	22	42	10	6	26	36	77	26	!

* Re-elected   ! Failed to gain re-election

SEASON	POSITION	P	W	D	L	F	A	Pts
Southern League								
1938 - 39	3	44	29	6	9	106	58	64
World War II								
1939 - 1944	League Competition suspended							
Kent League								
1944 - 45	1	18	14	1	3	77	38	29
1945 - 46	1	20	18	1	1	111	33	37
Southern League								
1946 - 47	1	32	21	5	6	103	45	47
1947 - 48	2	34	21	5	8	81	43	47
1948 - 49	1	42	26	10	6	104	48	62
1949 - 50	5	46	23	9	14	92	61	55

SEASON	POSITION	P	W	D	L	F	A	Pts
		Football League Division Three (South)						
1950 - 51	22	46	13	9	24	69	101	35
1951 - 52	22	46	11	13	22	71	81	35
1952 - 53	21	46	12	15	19	55	74	39
1953 - 54	10	46	19	10	17	61	66	48
1954 - 55	4	46	20	15	11	77	66	55
1955 - 56	10	46	19	10	17	69	71	48
1956 - 57	22	46	12	13	21	54	85	37
1957 - 58	22	46	13	9	24	52	81	35
		Football League Division Four						
1958 - 59	11	46	20	9	17	82	77	49
1959 - 60	7	46	21	10	15	74	69	52
1960 - 61	15	46	15	13	18	64	66	43
1961 - 62	20	44	13	11	20	73	94	37
1962 - 63	5	46	22	13	11	71	49	57
1963 - 64	1	46	23	14	9	59	30	60
		Football League Division Three						
1964 - 65	7	46	23	9	14	70	50	55
1965 - 66	6	46	22	8	16	62	54	52
1966 - 67	11	46	15	16	15	58	62	46
1967 - 68	12	46	18	12	16	59	63	48
1968 - 69	20	46	13	15	18	54	63	41
1969 - 70	20	46	13	13	20	52	64	39
1970 - 71	24	46	10	13	23	42	67	33
		Football League Division Four						
1971 - 72	13	46	16	13	17	61	67	45
1972 - 73	9	46	19	11	16	63	58	49
1973 - 74	2nd	46	25	12	9	90	49	62
		Football League Division Three						
1974 - 75	10th	46	17	14	15	65	60	48
1975 - 76	15th	46	12	19	15	58	68	43
1976 - 77	12th	46	16	12	18	55	64	44
1977 - 78	7th	46	15	20	11	67	60	50
1978 - 79	4th	46	21	17	8	65	42	59
1979 - 80	16th	46	14	14	18	49	51	42

GILLINGHAM'S POST-WAR RECORD IN THE F.A. CUP

Season	Round	Opponent	Venue	Score
1945 - 46	Fourth Qual. Round	Sutton United	Home	3 - 9
1946 - 47	Fourth Qual. Round	Guildford City	Away	2 - 1
	First Round	Gravesend and N.	Home	4 - 1
	Second Round	Bristol City	Away	2 - 1
	Third Round	Swansea	Away	1 - 4
1947 - 48	Fourth Qual. Round	Barnet	Home	3 - 1
	First Round	Leyton Orient	Home	1 - 0
	Second Round	Rochdale	Away	1 - 1
	Replay	Rochdale	Home	3 - 0
	Third Round	Q.P.R.	Home	1 - 1
	Replay	Q.P.R.	Away	1 - 3
1948 - 49	Fourth Qual. Round	Romford	Away	1 - 2
1949 - 50	Fourth Qual. Round	Guildford City	Away	3 - 2
	First Round	Hastings United	Away	3 - 1
	Second Round	Yeovil	Away	1 - 3
1950 - 51	First Round	Linby C.W.	Away	4 - 1
	Second Round	Bristol Rovers	Away	2 - 2
	Replay	Bristol Rovers	Home	1 - 1
	Second Replay	Bristol Rovers	!	1 - 2
1951 - 52	First Round	Crystal Palace	Away	1 - 0
	Second Round	Rochdale	Home	0 - 3
1952 - 53	First Round	Wellington	Away	1 - 1
	Replay	Wellington	Home	3 - 0
	Second Round	Stockport County	Away	1 - 3
1953 - 54	First Round	Walthamstow Ave.	Away	0 - 1
1954 - 55	First Round	Newport	Home	2 - 0
	Second Round	Reading	Home	1 - 1
	Replay	Reading	Away	3 - 5
1955 - 56	First Round	Shrewsbury	Home	1 - 1
	Replay	Shrewsbury	Away	1 - 4
1956 - 57	First Round	Yiewsley	Away	2 - 2
	Replay	Yiewsley	Home	2 - 0
	Second Round	Newport County	Home	1 - 2

! Played at White Hart Lane

Season	Round	Opponent	Venue	Score
1957 - 58	First Round	Gorleston	Home	10 - 1
	Second Round	Millwall	Away	1 - 1
	Replay	Millwall	Home	6 - 1
	Third Round	Nottingham Forest	Away	0 - 2
1958 - 59	First Round	Plymouth Argyle	Away	2 - 2
	Replay	Plymouth Argyle	Home	1 - 4
1959 - 60	First Round	Bedford Town	Away	4 - 0
	Second Round	Torquay United	Home	2 - 2
	Replay	Torquay United	Away	2 - 1
	Third Round	Swansea	Home	1 - 4
1960 - 61	First Round	Ashford Town	Away	2 - 1
	Second Round	Southend United	Home	3 - 2
	Third Round	Leyton United	Home	2 - 6
1961 - 62	First Round	Coventry City	Away	0 - 2
1962 - 63	First Round	Andover	Away	1 - 0
	Second Round	Bedford Town	Home	3 - 0
	Third Round	Port Vale	Home	2 - 4
1963 - 64	First Round	Q.P.R.	Away	1 - 4
1964 - 65	First Round	Guildford City	Away	2 - 2
	Replay	Guildford City	Home	1 - 0
	Second Round	Luton Town	Away	0 - 1
1965 - 66	First Round	Folkestone Town	Home	1 - 2
1966 - 67	First Round	Tamworth	Home	4 - 1
	Second Round	Walsall	Away	1 - 3
1967 - 68	First Round	Newport County	Away	0 - 3
1968 - 69	First Round	Orient	Away	1 - 1
	Replay	Orient	Home	2 - 1
	Second Round	Luton Town	Away	1 - 3
1969 - 70	First Round	Southend United	Away	0 - 0
	Replay	Southend United	Home	2 - 1
	Second Round	Tamworth	Home	6 - 0
	Third Round	Newport County	Home	1 - 0
	Fourth Round	Peterborough Utd.	Home	5 - 1
	Fifth Round	Watford	Away	1 - 2
1970 - 71	First Round	Brentford	Away	1 - 2
1971 - 72	First Round	Plymouth Argyle	Home	3 - 2
	Second Round	Romford	Away	1 - 0
	Third Round	Swansea City	Away	0 - 1
1972 - 73	First Round	Reading	Home	1 - 2
1973 - 74	First Round	Cambridge United	Away	2 - 3
1974 - 75	First Round	Hereford United	Away	0 - 1

1975 - 76	First Round	Weymouth	Away	2 - 0
	Second Round	Brighton	Home	0 - 1
1976 - 77	First Round	Watford	Home	0 - 1
1977 - 78	First Round	Weymouth	Home	1 - 1
	Replay	Weymouth	Away	1 - 0
	Second Round	Peterborough United	Home	1 - 1
	Replay	Peterborough United	Away	0 - 2
1978 - 79	First Round	Reading	Away	0 - 0
	Replay	Reading	Home	1 - 2
1979 - 80	First Round	Wimbledon	Home	0 - 0
	Replay	Wimbledon	Away	2 - 4

GILLINGHAM'S RECORD IN THE FOOTBALL LEAGUE CUP

1960 - 61	First Round	Bye		
	Second Round	Preston North End	Home	1 - 1
	Replay	Preston North End	Away	0 - 3
1961 - 62	First Round	Nottingham Forest	Away	1 - 4
1962 - 63	First Round	Newport County	Away	1 - 2
1963 - 64	First Round	Bristol City	Home	4 - 2
	Second Round	Bury	Home	3 - 0
	Third Round	Bristol Rovers	Away	1 - 1
	Replay	Bristol Rovers	Home	3 - 1
	Fourth Round	Leicester City	Away	1 - 3
1964 - 65	First Round	Exeter City	Away	0 - 2
1965 - 66	First Round	Bye		
	Second Round	Blackpool	Away	2 - 5
1966 - 67	First Round	Southend United	Away	0 - 0
	Replay	Southend United	Home	2 - 0
	Second Round	Arsenal	Away	1 - 1
	Replay	Arsenal	Home	1 - 1
	Replay	Arsenal	Away	0 - 5
1967 - 68	First Round	Orient	Away	3 - 1
	Second Round	Torquay United	Home	2 - 2
	Replay	Torquay United	Away	0 - 2
1968 - 69	First Round	Orient	Home	2 - 2
	Replay	Orient	Away	0 - 3
1969 - 70	First Round	Aldershot	Away	1 - 0
	Second Round	Blackpool	Away	1 - 3

Season	Round	Opponent	Venue	Score
1970 - 71	First Round	Luton Town	Home	0 - 1
1971 - 72	First Round	Reading	Home	4 - 0
	Second Round	Notts. County	Away	2 - 1
	Third Round	Grimsby Town	Home	1 - 1
	Replay	Grimsby Town	Away	0 - 1
1972 - 73	First Round	Colchester United	Home	1 - 0
	Second Round	Millwall	Home	0 - 2
1973 - 74	First Round	Colchester United	Home	4 - 2
	Second Round	Carlisle United	Home	1 - 2
1974 - 75	First Round	Bournemouth	Home	1 - 1
	Replay	Bournemouth	Away	1 - 1
	Second Replay	Bournemouth	*	1 - 2
1975 - 76	First Round	Reading	Away	1 - 0
		Reading	Home	1 - 1
1976 - 77	First Round	Aldershot	Away	1 - 1
		Aldershot	Home	2 - 1
	Second Round	Newcastle United	Home	1 - 2
1977 - 78	First Round	Wimbledon	Home	1 - 1
		Wimbledon	Away	1 - 1
1978 - 79	First Round	Reading	Away	1 - 3
		Reading	Home	1 - 2
1979 - 80	First Round	Luton Town	Home	3 - 0
		Luton Town	Away	1 - 1
	Second Round	Norwich City	Home	1 - 1
		Norwich City	Away	2 - 4

* Played at Brentford

From 1975 - 76 First Round played on a two legged basis and from 1979 - 80 the Second Round was also played on a two legged basis.

Helen.

Dennis Prouse (left) and Dave Pommeroy, the publicity men.

Linda.

Billy, the groundsman.

The Back-room 'Boys'.

Mamara, Triggs and Bradley, non-stop workers for the Club.

Some Photographs I Rather Liked

The music man.

Honestly I'll pay you that money . . .

In the cage.

Happiness is cleaning boots.

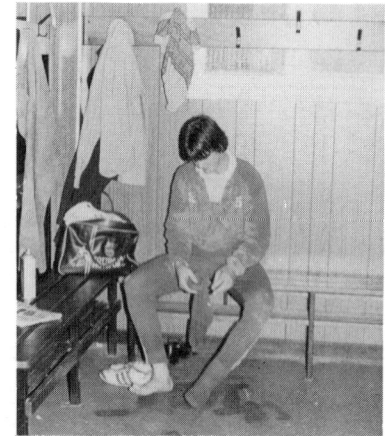
Found guilty of having a Tottenham Bag!

In the Hut.

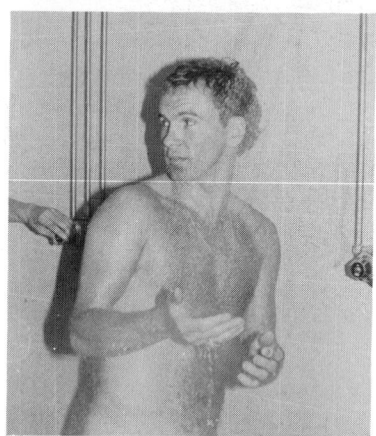
John Crabbe on his Birthday.

In the Box.

In the Box (2).

Richard Dennison
being mugged by Messrs Summers & Cox.

A dour Duncan.

The Fans

A Winter Watcher.

Young supporters get there early (just like Brian Moore did at their age)   The oldest supporter.

Nice try.

Different emotions of a near miss.

A lull on a Summers afternoon.

A Goal!!

... one for the other side?

Some work in the Summer to help out.

The Lads.

. . . and the Lassies.

Father & Son.

John Larcombe, a permanent Gills advertisement at his Cinema.

The late Terry Millan, an avid supporter who died whilst at an away match. The Away Supporters' Player of the Year Trophy bears his name, and was, last season won by John Crabbe.

The family at half-time.

THE PLAYERS

Full name	Richardson Damien John	Sharpe John William Henry	Sutton Gary	Walker Patrick	Weatherley Colin Mark	Westwood Daniel Robert	Wheatley Stephen John	White Dean
Date of birth	2.8.47	9.10.57	2.2.62	20.12.59	18.1.58	25.7.53	12.4.59	4.12.58
Birthplace	Dublin	Portsmouth	Folkestone	Dublin	Ramsgate	West Ham	Durham	Hastings
Birth sign	Leo	Libra	Aquarius	Sagittarius	Capricorn	Leo	Aries	Sagittarius
Height	5ft 11½in	5ft 11in	5ft 10in	5ft 8in	5ft 11in	5ft 10in	5ft 9in	5ft 11in
Weight	12 - 0	11 - 5	12.- 3	10 - 10	11 - 8	11 - 5	11 - 0	12 - 0
Previous clubs	Shamrock Rovers	Southampton	-	-	-	QPR	-	Chelsea
Date joined	27.10.72	2.10.78	31.7.78	23.5.76	15.12.75	9.1.76	3.5.77	18.7.78
Cost	£5,000	£25,000	-	-	-	£17,500	-	-
Previous jobs	Appt. radar mechanic	Schoolboy	Schoolboy	Schoolboy	Schoolboy	Ins. clerk	Floor tiler	Schoolboy
Wife's name	Rita	Liz	-	-	Pamela	Lynn Janet	Jean Marie	-
Interests outside football	Sports, music, reading	All sports	Sports, tropical fish	Sports, scenic drawing	Fishing	Cricket, golf	Gardening, all sports	Fishing
Pre match rituals	None	Ring, out last	-	Boot ritual	None	None	None	None
Nickname	Shamrock	Josh	The Hulk	-	Wev	-	Wheats	Chuck

Full name	Young Charles Frederick	Bottiglieri Antonio	Wakelin Nigel	Young David Alan	Doust Timothy Charles	Harrison Michael Joseph	Ford Andrew Carl	Henderson Peter	Lloyd Kevin
Date of birth	14.2.58	29.5.62	26.11.62	29.9.62	20.6.63	7.12.63	4.5.54	29.9.52	12.6.58
Birthplace	Nicosia	Chatham	Gravesend	Islington	London	Gateshead	Minehead	Berwick on Tweed	Wolverhampton
Birth sign	Aquarius	Gemini	Sagittarius	Libra	Gemini	Sagittarius	Taurus	Libra	Gemini
Height	6ft 1in	5ft 6in	5ft 9in	5ft 8in	5ft 10in	6ft	6ft	5ft 11½in	5ft 10in
Weight	11 - 2	10 - 6	10 - 7	10 - 0	11 - 1	11 - 7	12 - 0	11 - 10	11 - 6
Previous clubs	Aston Villa	-	-	-	-	-	Bournemouth Sthd/Swindon	Man.City Chester	Worcester Cardiff
Date joined	9.3.78	31.7.78	1.7.79	1.7.79	4.3.80	26.5.80	1.7.80	1.7.80	1.7.80
Cost	£35,000	-	-	-	-	-	£25,000	£30,000	-
Previous jobs	Schoolboy	Schoolboy	Schoolboy	Schoolboy	Schoolboy	Schoolboy	Schoolboy	P. Edtn. teacher	Roof tiler
Wife's name	-	-	-	-	-	-	Jenny	Susan Barbara	-
Interests outside football	All sports	Office managem't squash	Disco & jazz music	All sports	Music, Rugby, all sports	All sports	All sports	Music, films	All sports
Pre match rituals	-	-	Left boot first, same pads	Ankle pad on left ankle	Follow a forward out of dressing room	-	Left boot first	-	-
Nickname	-	'Botty'	Stick	-	-	-	-	Henders	-

Full name	Adams Michael Richard	Armstrong Gary	Barker Stephen Allan	Bruce Stephen	Crabbe Stephen John	Ford Colin	Donn Alan Nigel	Dudley Stephen
Date of birth	8.11.61	2.1.58	23.2.56	31.12.60	20.10.54	18.9.60	2.3.62	10.10.61
Birthplace	Sheffield	West Ham	Durham	Newcastle	Weymouth	London	Bearsted	Ramsgate
Birth sign	Scorpio	Capricorn	Pisces	Capricorn	Libra	Virgo	Pisces	Libra
Height	5ft 7in	5ft 8in	5ft 11½in	6ft	5ft 8in	5ft 8in	5ft 10in	5ft 8in
Weight	10 - 6	10 - 12	12 - 11	11 - 2	10 - 6	10 - 10	11 - 0	11 - 0
Previous clubs	Sheffield United	-	Newcastle	-	Southampt'n	-	-	-
Date joined	17.8.78	21.7.75	16.1.79	15.8.77	22.2.77	15.8.77	31.7.78	1.7.79
Cost			£40,000		£10,000			
Previous jobs	Schoolboy	Builder	Mechanic	Schoolboy	Schoolboy	Schoolboy	Schoolboy	Schoolboy
Wife's name	-	-	-	-	-	-	-	-
Interests outside football	Pigeon fancier	All sports	All sports	All sports	All sports	All sports	Cricket, golf	Cricket, golf
Pre match rituals	Left boot on first	Gold chain with bottle motif	-	-	-	Grandad's ring	Gold chain	-
Nickname	-	Stretch	Mickey	Brucey	Buster	-	Thatch	Duds

Full name	Duncan Colin John	Funnell Anthony	Hillyard Ronald William	Hughes Stephen John	Jolley Terence Arthur	Nicholl Terence John	Overton John	Price Kenneth
Date of birth	5.8.57	20.8.57	31.3.52	29.7.60	13.4.59	16.9.53	1.5.56	26.2.55
Birthplace	Plymouth	Eastbourne	Rotherham	Folkestone	London	Wilmslow	Rotherham	Wolverhampton
Birth sign	Leo	Leo	Aries	Leo	Aries	Virgo	Taurus	Pisces
Height	5ft 9in	5ft 7in	5ft 10½in	5ft 11in	5ft 11in	5ft 9½in	5ft 11in	5ft 10½in
Weight	11 - 5	10 - 10	11 - 0	12 - 0	11 - 0	11 - 6	11 - 10	12 - 2
Previous clubs	Oxford	Southampton	York	-	-	Crewe, Sheff. Unt., Sthd.	Aston Villa	Southend
Date joined	31.1.80	29.3.79	4.7.74	19.7.76	5.7.76	22.12.76	25.5.76	22.12.76
Cost	£50,000	£40,000	-	-	-	£6,000	-	£2,000
Previous jobs	Schoolboy	Labourer	-	Schoolboy	Schoolboy	Apprentice engineer	Schoolboy	Elect. engineer
Wife's name	-	Hilary	Susan	-	-	Stephanie	Helen	Cora
Interests outside football	Golf	Golf, tennis	Squash, golf	All sports, music	All sports, music	Football coaching, music	All sports, music	Sea-fishing, shooting, golf
Pre match rituals	-	-	None	None	None	Total silence at home	Last to leave dressing room	-
Nickname	Dunc	Ferret	Sambo	Billy	Drac	-	Ovy	-

Epilogue

This is a misnomer. There is not and will not be an epilogue to a Club which has given, over its eighty-seven years, joy and heartache to millions. Each new season is a new chance, with hope and frustration, passion and agony all expected by those thousands who will be going to see 'The Blues'. This is what the supporters (that's you and me) expect; vicious and aggressive, passive and loving we are all far more 'prima donna-ish' than the players.

At the end of the 19th Century some men got together and started it all off. Although they are long dead and forgotten, their efforts have borne fruit and I think they would be proud of their prodigy.

I have tried in this short work to give the flavour of the Club, which is a human entity, but, to interpolate on Dr. Grossmark's words, we always have to think about tomorrow, and that is the wonder of the game. Always there is a tomorrow and by the time you read these words they are old fashioned. Already the games of 1980/81 are being engraved in Gillingham's Folk Lore; the penalties, the sending offs, goals and missed chances are now being debated in public houses and front rooms throughout the Medway and even further afield. The Press will be interviewing the stars and analysing every move and no doubt Gerry Summers will retain his bad memory . . . New styles. . . New faces . . . but that's football.

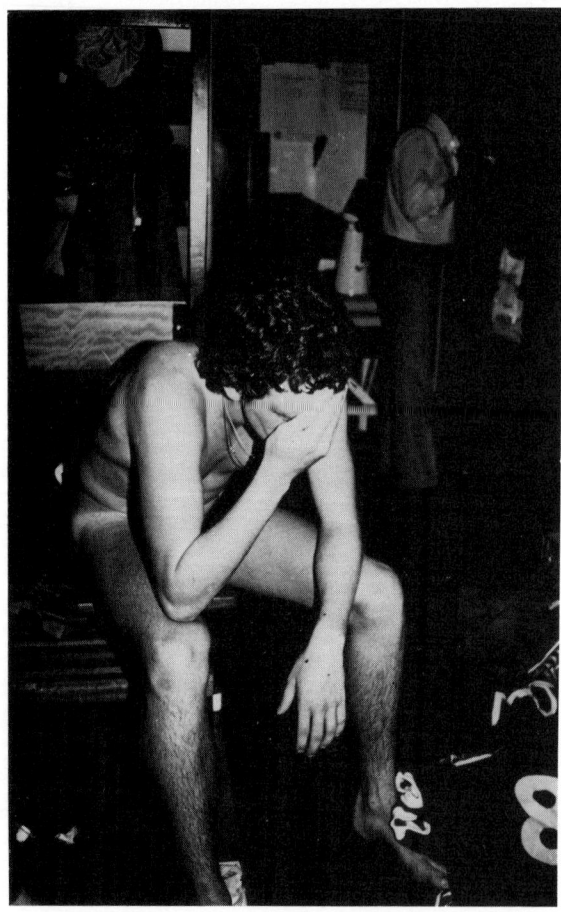

Exhaustion – (Steve Bruce).

Meresborough Books

PUBLISHERS AND WHOLESALERS OF BOOKS ON KENT
7 STATION ROAD, RAINHAM, GILLINGHAM, KENT. ME8 7RS
Telephone Medway (0634) 371591

BYGONE KENT. A monthly journal on all aspects of Kent History. 95p per month. Annual Subscription £10.50. A free sample copy will be sent on request.

VILLAGES AROUND OLD MAIDSTONE by Irene Hales. Over 140 old postcards depicting the villages in a seven mile radius around Maidstone. £2.50 (£2.80 post free).

US BARGEMEN by A. S. Bennett. A new book of sailing barge life around Kent and Essex from the author of 'June of Rochester' and 'Tide Time'. £6.95 (£7.50 post free).

A VIEW OF CHRIST'S COLLEGE, BLACKHEATH by A.E.O. Crombie, B.A., Master, Headmaster and Tutor 1920-1976. £6.95 (£7.95 post free).

A NEW DICTIONARY OF KENT DIALECT by Alan Major. All the words from Parish and Shaw's Dictionary of 1888 are included, but many more have been added from a wide variety of sources. Publication January, 1981. £7.50 (£7.95 post free)

THE GILLS by Tony Conway. A history of Gillingham Football Club. 96 large format pages packed with old photographs. Hardback. £5.95 (£6.95 post free).

KENT CASTLES by John Guy. The first comprehensive guide to all the castles and castle sites in Kent. The first part outlines the history of castles and castle building. The second part gives the history of over 60 castles in Kent with a guide for the modern visitor. 264 pages. Over 150 illustrations. Hardback. £7.50 (£7.95 post free).

THE CANTERBURY AND WHITSTABLE RAILWAY 1930-1980: A PICTORIAL SURVEY. (Published with the Locomotive Club of Great Britain.) 28 pages. Over 30 pictures and maps. 75p (95p post free).

MEDWAY MEMORIES by Norman Clout. A series of talks first broadcast on Radio Medway, Summer 1980. £1.50 (£.180 post free).

ROCHESTER'S HERITAGE TRAIL. (Published for The City of Rochester Society). A useful guide for the visitor to most places of interest in Rochester. 95p (£1.15 post free).

OLD MAIDSTONE by Kay Baldock and Irene Hales. Over 100 old postcards from the early years of this century. 52 large format pages. £1.95 (£2.25 post free).

WATERMILLS AND WINDMILLS OF KENT by William Coles Finch. The classic book on all Kent mills reprinted at £10.00, now available at £4.95 (£5.95 post free).

STROOD A PICTORIAL HISTORY by Avril Bloomfield. Over 100 fascinating old photographs. Hardback £2.95 (£3.35 post free).